Reconstruction Era and Gilded Age

A Captivating Guide to a Period in US History That Greatly Impacted American Civil Rights and an Era of Rapid Economic Growth

Free Bonus from Captivating History
(Available for a Limited time)

Hi History Lovers!

Now you have a chance to join our exclusive history list so you can get your first history ebook for free as well as discounts and a potential to get more history books for free! Simply visit the link below to join.

Captivatinghistory.com/ebook

Also, make sure to follow us on Facebook, Twitter and Youtube by searching for Captivating History.

Contents

Part 1: The Reconstruction Era

A Captivating Guide to a Period in the History of the United States of America That Greatly Impacted American Civil Rights after the War for Southern Independence

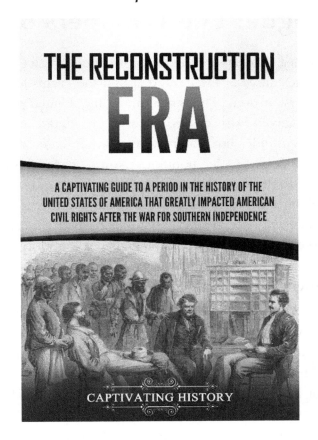

Prologue: The Whispers of War

Before we begin to explore the Reconstruction Era, let's look more closely at the causes of the Civil War and the events leading up to the war's first action. The situation in the United States when Abraham Lincoln was elected to the presidency can only be described as a tinder box waiting to explode in flames. There were many issues between the populous North, whose economy was thriving due to the rising industries, and the South, whose economy was based on millions of slaves. Although Northerners could be quite prejudiced, the Northern states abolished slavery by 1804. Besides their difference in opinions when it came to slavery, the Southerners also resented what they saw as unfair taxation from the federal government and the denial of states' rights.

There was also another major issue facing the Union: what to do with the new territories. Of course, each side wanted the new states that were admitted to the Union to coincide with their beliefs on slavery. The Missouri Compromise of 1850 helped placate the people for a time, but the Kansas-Nebraska Act of 1854 rekindled tensions, culminating in "Bleeding Kansas," which was essentially a civil war within Kansas. Some refer to it as the overture to the Civil War.

Abraham Lincoln, a Republican, was elected as the sixteenth president in 1860. While Lincoln ran on a platform that called for the limitation of slavery, he did not seek to dismantle the institution in states where it already existed because the practice of slavery was supported by the Constitution. However, the South feared that this would change and that Lincoln would approve of policies that would eventually dismantle slavery while favoring the business practices of the North.

The Southerners were not entirely wrong, as Lincoln favored the benefits that came from the Industrial Revolution. Unfortunately, these benefits did not flow below the Mason-Dixon line (the informal boundary line between the free North and the slave states in the South). The Industrial Revolution never really took off in the agricultural South, as 90 percent of the country's manufacturing economy was in the North by 1860.

The South mainly depended on the cotton trade, which grew exponentially with the invention of the cotton gin. Most of their cotton was exported; in fact, the South produced two-thirds of the world's cotton during this time. With this boom in the cotton trade came the demand for more slaves. It also increased the disparity between the whites in the South, as few ever became rich enough to own a large plantation that employed many slaves. Yet despite their monetary differences, white Southerners managed to hold onto the same belief that slavery was advantageous for all and that the blacks who toiled in the fields were lesser than they were.

So even though the South lagged far behind the North on the industrial side of things, it was not all bleak for the South when the Civil War broke out. The South had tremendous wealth in the slave-run economy. In 1860, slaves were worth more than all of the North's banks, factories, and railroads combined. Cotton was also a worldwide export crop, which led the Confederate leaders to expect economic, military, and diplomatic assistance in the war from European countries. Although the North had an estimated 3.5

million able-bodied men in comparison to the South's 1 million men (excluding slaves), the Southerners had much more experience in fighting. But perhaps most important of all, the Southerners were united in their beliefs. Not all Northerners were invested enough in the issue of slavery to go to war and die for people who they saw as inferior. It is possible these factors led to overconfidence in the Confederacy.

On December 20th, 1860, South Carolina officially seceded from the United States. Other states started to follow suit, and before Lincoln was inaugurated in March 1861, seven states had seceded the Union. These seven states established the Confederate States of America in February 1861, and little over a month later, the South would attack Fort Sumter, signaling the beginning of the Civil War.

Introduction

After the Civil War ended in 1865, there was much that needed to be addressed. The rights of the freed blacks, how to incorporate those Southern states that reentered the Union, and the economy, among many other issues, all had to be evaluated.

The Reconstruction era sought to fix these issues and lay down the groundwork for a better tomorrow. However, while the government managed to unite the country once again, it failed to solve the crisis that blacks faced in the South and in the country as a whole. One could draw a direct line from the Reconstruction's failure in this arena to the racism in America today.

But what caused it to fail? What is the legacy of the Reconstruction in America today? Together, we will walk along the road from Washington, DC, to Mississippi. We will journey from Lincoln's idealist vision of putting the Union back together to Andrew Johnson's Reconstruction policies to the election of 1876. During this time, three constitutional amendments were passed in about five years. That is quite a feat. And in the midst of passing these amendments, Congress also passed the Civil Rights Act of 1866, the Reconstruction Act of 1867, the Ku Klux Klan Act, and the Civil Rights Act of 1875. However, the election of 1876 effectively ended both the Reconstruction and Lincoln's dream of an America "filled with our better angels."

There were some good things that came from the Reconstruction, such as public schools for African Americans, the end of slavery, and the African Americans' right to vote. Blacks could own property and enter into contracts. However, these laws were great on paper, but they didn't meet their full potential in reality.

The good was met with the bad. In response to the Union's integration of blacks into the nation, the South passed restrictive laws known as the Black Codes in 1865 and 1866. This behavior led to the emergence of the Radical Republicans, who believed the abolition of slavery didn't go far enough. These Republicans pushed for even more equitable reforms.

Since the civil rights movement of the 1960s, we have celebrated every "first" black governor, black congressman, black senator, and black state legislators. The truth is there were a number of African Americans in state legislatures and even in Congress between 1867 and the end of the Reconstruction. In the years that followed, white Southerners drove them out with the implementation of the Jim Crow laws and voter suppression tactics. The civil rights movement didn't introduce these "radical ideas" of African Americans holding office. During the Reconstruction, black legislators not only existed—they flourished. Blacks holding public office was fairly common until the Ku Klux Klan's rebirth drove blacks back into living under a second-class status.

After examining the events and milestones of the Reconstruction, there will be a short review of the Supreme Court 1896 doctrine of "separate but equal" in the landmark case of *Plessy v. Ferguson*. This decision stood for decades, and it short-changed thousands of children of color in their education.

At the end of the day, the failure of the Reconstruction was not in the legislation and amendments. It was in the implementation or rather non-implementation of these laws. The country's leaders wanted to obtain their political goals, and in the process, they sacrificed important policies that would have benefited the freed blacks.

Chapter 1 – The Civil War

The year is 1865. America had been tearing itself apart for four years by this point. For many decades before the war broke out, the Northern and Southern states had argued intensely over three essential points. These were slavery, westward expansion, and states' rights in a time of a growing federal government.

When Abraham Lincoln won the presidency in 1860, these arguments boiled over. Initially, there were only seven states in the Confederate States of America, but by May 1861, there were eleven states. However, Lincoln was determined to hold the Union together without losing any state permanently to the Confederacy.

Jefferson Davis became the president of the Confederate States of America, with Alexander Stephens as the vice president. Davis was a war veteran, and he also served as the secretary of war from 1853 to 1857. Stephens was a Georgia representative, and he made what is known as the Cornerstone Speech in 1861. In this speech, Stephens introduced the Confederate Constitution and proclaimed that white supremacy was the "cornerstone" of the Confederacy. He stated that the "peculiar institution of African slavery was the immediate cause of the late rupture [of the Union] and present revolution."

Like most of the other Southerners, Stephens did not believe that "all men are created equal," as the United States Constitution declared. He thought that "those ideas...were fundamentally wrong." Stephens proclaimed, "The foundations are laid, its cornerstone rests, upon the great truth that the negro is not equal to the white man." Stephens firmly believed that for "Black Americans, slavery subordination to the superior race is his natural and normal condition."

Stephens made it very clear in his speech that the continuation and expansion of slavery was the cause of the secession and the war itself. And he was certainly not the only one to think so. For example, when Mississippi seceded, their declaration stated, "Our position is thoroughly identified with the institution of slavery—the greatest material interest of the world." In other words, Mississippi announced that saving the institution of slavery justified a civil war. Their declaration of secession went on to say, "Its labor supplies the product which constitutes by far the largest and most important portions of the commerce of the earth...A blow at slavery is a blow at commerce and civilization."

However, not everyone in the South felt this way, or at least they were not willing to separate from the Union over their beliefs on the matter. A great example of this can be seen in the case of West Virginia. In 1861, Virginia voted on whether or not to secede. Many in the northwestern part of Virginia voted against the referendum. They broke away from the main state of Virginia, which seceded from the Union. In 1863, West Virginia was officially declared a state. It became a critical border state, and it was one of two states admitted to the Union during the Civil War, with the other one being Nevada. However, not everyone was happy with statehood, as there were many slave owners in the southern part of West Virginia. In a way, the conflict in Virginia was a microcosm of the nationwide conflict.

There were a lot of famous battles and figures that arose during the Civil War, but this book is only going to provide a brief description of its end. In 1864, Major General Ulysses S. Grant was appointed as the Union Army's lieutenant general. This decision was perhaps one of the most important of the war. Between Grant and General William Tecumseh Sherman, the Union Army was able to put the Confederate troops on the run and force a surrender. Grant's nine-month siege of Petersburg led to Confederate General Robert E. Lee's retreat. During those nine months, Sherman led his infamous "March to the Sea," during which he burned much of Georgia to the ground. South Carolina fell to Sherman in February 1865, followed by North Carolina. Following the siege on Petersburg, Grant pursued Lee's forces to Appomattox, where Lee surrendered to him.

Unfortunately, Abraham Lincoln was assassinated before the Confederate States of America officially surrendered (however, it should be noted that the war was effectively over once Lee surrendered). John Wilkes Booth, a Southern sympathizer, took matters into his own hands on the fateful day of April 14th, shooting the president while he was enjoying a play. On May 9th, 1865, the Civil War came to a close.

It was a very unfortunate turn of events when President Lincoln was assassinated. The South's strong feelings against Lincoln led Booth to decide it was his duty to eliminate the president. There is little doubt among historians that if Lincoln had lived, the Reconstruction would have been very different. Perhaps there would have been more healing and better relationships between the people.

The Civil War lasted about four years and took the lives of between 616,000 and 1.5 million soldiers. The North proved victorious in the end, so new states added to the Union could no longer even consider implementing slavery. However, war comes with a price, and this price was most certainly felt in the South, as it was essentially a wasteland at the end of the war.

The North won the war for many reasons, but the economic changes it implemented and its burgeoning industrial economy were significant factors. The agricultural and slave-driven economy of the South could not produce the supplies, weapons, and support that the North could. It also could not compete with the manpower of the North.

President Andrew Johnson, who took over after Lincoln was assassinated, would reunite the Union after the South's surrender. Still, much bitterness remains to this day. The South saw its economy destroyed and its land and the families who inhabited it devasted. Union forces had burned the cities of the South to the ground, and there was widespread hunger and homelessness. This bitterness would live on in the oppression of freed blacks in the South.

However, there was just as much bitterness on the part of the North toward the South. For many in the North, slavery was a moral abomination. The thought that the South had killed their president was embedded in Northern attitudes. Still, the Union attempted to show mercy to the Confederate Army, imprisoning few and only executing one.

The South's bitterness only increased, though, and it was fortified by the punishing and humiliating Reconstruction. Thousands of Southerners lost all of their savings and income when the war ended, as the Confederacy's currency and government securities were suddenly without value.

The scene was set for the Reconstruction era, which had lasting effects on the United States of America. As the post-war era began, the South was already suffering from a very shaky economy. The Emancipation Proclamation of 1862, which freed the slaves in the Confederate states, helped to wipe out the unpaid labor force in the South, causing both economic and philosophical pain and anger.

The Emancipation Proclamation was not the only legislation passed during the war that allowed the Union to increase its economic and military advantages. Six essential pieces of legislation were passed during the Civil War: the Homestead Act, the Morrill Act (also known as the Land-Grant College Act), the Pacific Railway Act, the Legal Tender Act, the Internal Revenue Act, and the National Bank Act. To better understand the position the North was in at the end of the war, it is necessary to take a deeper look into these acts.

The Homestead Act

Since the early 1840s, Congress had debated the ideas behind the Homestead Act. This legislature was very popular in the North, but the Southern politicians were skeptical and worried that new territory would be free of slavery. The Homestead Act was finally passed once the Southern delegation had departed the Union in May of 1862.

The Homestead Act offered 160 acres to anyone willing to move to the West. The main condition for receiving this land was that it had to be improved upon, as the US government wanted to foster growth in the Western territories. The passage of this act allowed free white farmers, as well as freed blacks, to make their living off the land, blocking the large plantation owners of the South from expanding and utilizing slaves to work in the fields.

The Morrill Act (the Land-Grant College Act)

This act, which was passed in July 1862, created colleges and universities by using the proceeds from federal land sales. Some of the colleges that were created due to this act are among the best in the US even today. The Morrill Act granted each state a tract of land to endow A&M colleges (Agricultural and Mechanical colleges). These schools were designed to give students in the lower classes an opportunity to receive higher education. They were also given the task of developing better farm equipment and better processes for future agricultural success.

Each of these schools was required to teach mechanical arts, agriculture, and military tactics. A good example of a famous A&M college today is Texas A&M, which has a well-known cadet program.

Before the Morrill Act was passed, higher education in the US was quite different. Universities often taught classical studies, which required the knowledge of dead languages, barring the working classes from attending. The Southerners in Congress often hailed from affluent families, and many of them wanted to keep the wealth in their own hands, so the act was only able to be passed once they seceded from the Union. When the act first passed, it only applied to those states that did not secede, but in time, it grew to include all the states in the Union.

The Pacific Railway Act

Since people were moving westward following the Homestead Act, it only seemed reasonable to build a transcontinental railroad. In July of 1862, President Lincoln signed the Pacific Railway Act, which aimed to link the East with the underdeveloped West.

Before secession, this was a hot topic along regional lines, as Northerners wanted the railroad to travel a northern route while the Southerners battled for a southern route. Following the departure of the Democrats, the Republican Congress devised a middle path that quickly passed both Houses. The railroad would start at Council Bluffs, Missouri, and end at Sacramento, California.

The construction of this transcontinental railroad was a godsend for Northern factories and workers. Thousands were able to get jobs, while the South was, for the most part, left out. This was probably not only due to the South seceding from the Union but also because building the railroad was an industrial job, and Southerners had minimal industrial experience. The railroad linked the uncharted West with established cities in the East, leaving behind the South, at least for now.

Financial Legislation

The next three pieces of legislation belong to the country's financial realm. They established standards and laws that we still follow today. However, each of these acts was a thorn in the South's side.

The Legal Tender Act

The first of these acts was the Legal Tender Act. It gave the federal government the power to print and use paper money to pay for the war. Until this act, it had been policy to only use gold and silver to pay for government actions. This would allow the use of paper money when the reserves of silver and gold were depleted. The bill aimed to finance the war without raising taxes, and it worked incredibly well. Even though the so-called "greenbacks" were not backed by silver or gold in similar amounts, businesses were still required by law to accept the greenbacks at face value. Due to its success, these paper notes paved the way for a national currency in the United States. The Union printed around 450 million dollars during the war.

The Internal Revenue Act

The North struggled to finance the war, and in 1861, the Revenue Act was passed. It was the first income tax ever levied on the public, placing more of the burden on the shoulders of the wealthy. However, before the first income tax was ever collected, the US government passed the second Revenue Act in 1862. This adjusted the income tax, separating the taxpayers into levels based on their incomes. It also established the predecessor for the Internal Revenue Service (IRS) and levied excise taxes on the people, which greatly affected lower-income Americans.

The National Bank Act

The National Bank Act, which was passed in 1863, was an attempt to create a federal bank. It delineated a plan to create a single federal currency and a system of national banks, which would counter the smaller, local banks. This act was particularly abhorrent to the South, as they emphasized states' rights and limited federal rule. They knew that national banks would be more tightly regulated by the government. This act improved the Union's financial situation, but it did not cure its financial ills.

The Southerners believed in a small federal government and strong state control. The agricultural and slavery-driven economy of the South did not lend itself to any strong central government or financial organization. This type of economy turned out to be a significant disadvantage in the war. The South could not build the same financial programs as the North, so it was not set up for success and growth after the war ended.

The Condition of the Union after the War

President Andrew Johnson faced the massive challenge of bringing the Confederate states back into the Union and integrating around four million freed slaves into society. The South was decimated with no currency and no workforce.

In 1861, 297 cities and towns in the Confederacy had a population of around 835,000. At some point during the war, any city or town with a population of over 681,000 had Union forces occupying them. Sherman's March to the Sea involved burning Atlanta to the ground and destroying Charleston, Richmond, and Columbia. Smaller towns suffered less damage, but they were still economically devastated.

On the plantations and farms, 40 percent of the mules, horses, and cattle were killed. In addition to the destruction of land and animals, there was also damage done to the farmers' machines and farming implements. The war destroyed the architecture and infrastructure of the South. Riverboats and railroads were in short supply due to the Southern policy of destroying them as they retreated. Even if they had crops and animals to sell, very little could be moved to market.

Most of the rest of the transportation system, including bridges, rail yards, rolling transportation stock, and repair shops, was also in disrepair. When the Union Army moved through the South, they destroyed anything they could.

Between the loss of human lives, physical destruction, and the overwhelming expense of the war, the South was in a poor state. The Confederacy had also run up a total debt of over 1.4 billion dollars. The Confederate dollar was worthless, and its banking system was failing. Bartering became the currency of the post-war South, as the economic system as a whole had to be rebuilt, this time without slave labor. Due to the war, many plantation owners had little money to pay for the labor of freed blacks. This situation led to the sharecropper economy. Former slaves became sharecroppers, living on the land and working it but paying the majority of their profits to the landowners. The economy changed from wealthy plantation owners to agricultural tenant farmers.

The end of the war also brought about a large migration to the North. Freed people moved to the urban areas in droves, taking any jobs they could find, mostly in the service industry or a sector that required unskilled labor. Black women largely engaged in domestic work and remained there for generations. They took care of white children, cleaned homes, took in laundry, or became cooks. Men worked in lumber mills, on the railroads, and in hotels.

Meanwhile, the white population in the South was decimated, as almost 25 percent of the young men were killed. These men were the breadwinners for their families, which meant many were driven into poverty. All of these factors locked the South into a multigenerational cycle of poverty, and these were the challenges that faced the Union government during the Reconstruction era.

The damage was not nearly as devastating in the North, although there had been a massive loss of life there as well. The North lost more people than the South, but the North's population was also far greater, even before the migration of the freed people. It is believed the North suffered over 828,000 (over 365,000 dead) casualties, while the South had around 864,000 (over 290,000 dead). This includes dead, wounded, captured, and missing.

At one point during the war, the Union was spending nearly one million dollars per week. Overall expenditures can only be estimated, but Claudia Goldin and Frank Lewis have made the best estimations to date in their report, "The Economic Cost of the American Civil War: Estimates and Implications," which was written in 1975. The following monetary costs were included:

For the North:

Government expenditures were around 2.3 billion dollars.

The loss of human capital was around 1.1 billion dollars.

Property loss was zero for the North.

For the South:

Government expenditures were around 1 billion dollars.

The loss of human capital was around 767 million dollars.

Property loss was 1.5 billion for the South.

In his last speech before he died, Lincoln discussed the possibility of giving freed blacks and those who had served in the military the right to vote. Four days later, Lincoln was assassinated. Lincoln had an idea of how he wanted the Reconstruction efforts to take shape. Instead, the role was suddenly thrust upon Andrew Johnson. Let's take a look at how Lincoln envisioned Reconstruction.

Chapter 2 – Lincoln's Vision

One of Lincoln's greatest visions actually occurred during the Civil War; this was the famous Emancipation Proclamation. The other piece of his vision that never came to fruition was something known as the Ten Percent Plan.

The Emancipation Proclamation

An incredible thing happened on September 22nd, 1862, in the United States of America. This had an impact on both the Union and the Confederacy, and it had long-reaching implications for the nation as a whole.

What was this incredible thing? On September 22nd, 1862, President Abraham Lincoln courageously issued an executive order. On January 1st, 1863, all slaves held in bondage in the Confederacy would forever be free. Even more critical were the phrases in this presidential proclamation that stated this freedom would be recognized and protected by the United States military.

The Emancipation Proclamation was something abolitionists had been dreaming of for decades. The Fugitive Slave Act of 1850 struck a severe blow to abolitionism, as it required runaway slaves to be returned to their owners even if they managed to cross into a state that no longer had slavery. When the Civil War broke out,

Lincoln wanted this law gone, mainly because it implied the Confederacy was a separate nation that had to be respected.

The Dred Scott case of 1857 set black people back even more. Dred Scott was a slave whose owners took him from the slave-holding state of Missouri into Illinois, where slavery was illegal. Scott sued for his freedom, but the US Supreme Court ruled that the US Constitution did not include black people when they used the term "citizens." By June of 1862, both Congress and Lincoln were prepared to defy this Supreme Court decision. Lincoln had been worried about going against the Constitution and dismantling slavery during his presidential run, but he ultimately signed the legislation passed by Congress, outlawing slavery in all of the current Union states and any future states. This action confined slavery to the states where it already existed. Congress then passed the Confiscation Act of 1862 in July of the same year. This legislation set up a process for freeing slaves owned by convicted rebels or those abandoning the Union Army. Of course, these actions alienated the Confederate states even more and laid the groundwork for the Emancipation Proclamation.

Lincoln freed the slaves with the Emancipation Proclamation; well, he at least freed the slaves in the Confederate States of America. Those slaves who lived in the border states were still stuck in the same position as before. These states were Maryland, Kentucky, Delaware, Missouri, and West Virginia. It was thought that if the slaves were freed in these states, the people might turn to the Confederacy, putting the North in a more precarious position. However, of the four million slaves in the nation, more than three and a half million slaves were granted their freedom under this federal law. Eventually, either federal or state actions freed the slaves in the border states as well.

From this point onward, any slave who found their way across Union lines or living in an area liberated by Union soldiers was permanently and immediately free. When the North won the war, all slaves everywhere were freed with the passage of the Thirteenth Amendment, which was ratified in December of 1865.

The Republican drive to free the slaves during the Civil War was egged on by the Northern press. In one notable incident, the *New-York Tribune* ran an editorial by Horace Greeley, who called for the end to slavery in all the states. Greeley stated that slavery would continue to present a danger to the Union even after the war ended. In response, Lincoln maintained that his only duty was to save the Union, even if that meant slavery still existed. Despite saying this publicly, Lincoln was morally opposed to slavery and desired to free the people held in bondage. Lincoln's response was posited to soften any white opposition in the North who didn't support the idea of abolition by tying it to the Union's survival.

In fact, Lincoln had already drafted a preliminary proclamation before he even addressed Greeley's concerns. US historian Todd Brewster believes that Lincoln sought to end slavery but realized he needed to frame it in a way that would sit well with the American public. By using a war-related proclamation to free the slaves in the rebel states, Lincoln and his attorney general believed they could remain free, regardless of the decision in the Dred Scott case.

Even though the Emancipation Proclamation is remembered best for doing the right and moral thing by setting the slaves in the Confederacy free, it can also be seen as a military move, as the Emancipation Proclamation allowed freed slaves to join the Union Army, giving the North an additional source of manpower. However, they often weren't given combat roles and were instead given hard, dirty tasks, like digging trenches. They were not paid as much as white soldiers, and they were often given poorer equipment. Despite this, black people joined the army in droves, as they were fighting for something they held dear, and it is believed that blacks made up 10 percent of the Union Army. Black people also helped to feed soldiers and repaired anything from railroads to uniforms. In addition to that, they also worked in many areas of the Northern economy.

When Lincoln issued the Emancipation Proclamation, he understood that freeing all the slaves would require a constitutional amendment since the proclamation only dealt with those states in the Confederacy. Lincoln worked on a series of amendments to make the process of abolition smoother, but none of them passed. By the time January 1ˢᵗ, 1863, rolled around, the Emancipation Proclamation was in effect, forever changing history in the United States. Although those in the North were hopeful for a brighter future, there was still a lot of resentment in both halves of the country.

In May 1863, the Confederacy passed their own legislation, calling for "full and ample retaliation" against the Union. They were worried that the sight of black men in uniform would stir something inside the slaves, something that would inspire them to throw off their chains and fight back. Before this legislation was passed, members of the Confederate Congress even suggested killing all captured Union soldiers, whether they were black or white. In the end, it was decided that black soldiers fighting for the Union who were captured by the Confederacy would be treated as runaway slaves. The Confederacy even increased the price for a slave after the Emancipation Proclamation because they believed there would be even more support for slavery in the South.

Part of Lincoln's plan for the Reconstruction included a requirement for every Southern state to abolish slavery by state law. Without this law in place, the state could not reenter the Union. His post-war plan also included the passage of the Thirteenth Amendment, which was ultimately passed and ended slavery in the United States.

The Emancipation Proclamation and the Gettysburg Address (the speech he gave at the dedication of the Soldiers' National Cemetery) are perhaps the most memorable moments of Lincoln's presidential career.

The Ten Percent Plan

The Emancipation Proclamation radically changed what was at stake in the war. If the Union won under these conditions, it would create a major social revolution in the Southern states once they returned to the fold. In light of this, Lincoln spent most of his time considering how to reunite the rebel states with the Union. How could Reconstruction bring the Union closer together rather than allowing the bitterness to divide it more?

Once Lincoln saw that the Union was moving toward total victory, he turned his attention to this challenge. Since Lincoln believed the South never "legally" seceded, he wanted the Reconstruction to be forgiving and not punitive. It was along these lines that he issued the Proclamation of Amnesty and Reconstruction in early December 1863.

This proclamation was built on the foundation of the Emancipation Proclamation, and it offered the rebel states a conciliatory way to rejoin the Union. Lincoln had no desire to punish the rebel states; after all, his goal from the beginning of the war was focused on saving the *entire* Union.

There were three major points in this proclamation.

> • A full pardon would be granted to everyone involved in the rebellion, including the restoration of their property. The only exception was the top-level Confederate Army officers and the top-level civilian officials of the Confederate government. Lincoln promised the rejoining Southerners that he would protect their private property except for their slaves.

- When ten percent of all eligible voters in the Confederate States of America sworn allegiance to the United States, a new state government could be formed.

- The states that participated in the first two steps were then to design and enact plans for integrating the freed slaves into the community without compromising their liberties.

In time, this proclamation became better known as the Ten Percent Plan. It was a plan that the South could have swallowed without a lot of rancor and bitterness, and it was a much more charitable plan than most people on both sides had expected. Perhaps it was too generous.

Some in Congress bowed to Lincoln's power and prestige, saying they believed the Ten Percent Plan would end the war and reunite the nation quickly. Lincoln believed this as well, for he feared the longer the war went on, the lower the chance of reuniting the Union. In his mind, the proclamation was actually an enticement for the South to surrender. He was also worried about the upcoming election in 1864; if the Democrats regained control, all of his work would be undone.

Lincoln's vision included a self-reconstruction by the reunited states. In other words, the federal government would not have a significant role or offer major assistance in their post-Civil War efforts. Three states rejoined the Union by 1864: Louisiana, Tennessee, and Arkansas. Louisiana promised its citizens many benefits for rejoining the Union peacefully. These benefits included public works projects, public schools for all without cost, and improvements to labor systems. Louisiana also abolished slavery, although it did not give the right to vote to the freed slaves.

However, not all in Congress agreed with this plan. The Radical Republicans wanted more punitive measures taken against the South, including the disbandment of the planter aristocracy. The Radical Republicans held the minority, but they managed to introduce a bill to the floor that held some support, which will be covered in the next chapter.

Chapter 3 – The Wade-Davis Bill and the Radical Republicans

During the Civil War, there were two opposing camps within the Republican Party. On one side, there was Abraham Lincoln and the moderates, and on the other side were the Radical Republicans. For Lincoln and the moderates, it was vital to handle Reconstruction as quickly as possible and get the Union reunited. However, the Radical Republicans wanted to see slavery completely and immediately destroyed, no matter the cost.

The Republican Party was split into moderates and Radicals from around 1854 until 1877, the year Reconstruction ended. Most Radical Republicans were inspired by religious or moral institutions that saw slavery as evil. Many of them were Christians and/or were a part of the abolitionist movements in the US. The more extreme Christians believed that the Civil War was a punishment from God for the sin of slavery.

Some of the most prominent Radical Republicans included William H. Seward, the US secretary of state under Lincoln and Johnson; Thaddeus Stevens, a US congressman from Pennsylvania;

and Horace Greeley, a newspaper editor. There were many other influential people who sided with the Radicals, such as Ulysses S. Grant, Edwin Stanton, John A. Logan, and Benjamin Butler.

Thaddeus Stevens was perhaps the most notable leader of the Radical Republicans. Stevens had been an ardent abolitionist for many years. Before entering Congress, Stevens was a Pennsylvania lawyer with many freedom-seeking clients. Once in Congress, he chaired the House Ways and Means Committee and was one of the House's most influential members. During the war, Stevens constantly prodded Lincoln on the issue of freeing the slaves. He did not believe the Confederate states should reenter the Union without meeting rigid requirements. In fact, Stevens viewed the seceded states as conquered provinces.

While Stevens piloted the House, Charles Sumner led the Radical Republicans in the Senate. Sumner had no qualms in making his stance known, and he once paid the price for it. In an anti-slavery speech he gave in 1856, Sumner called a South Carolina senator a "pimp for slavery," and his first cousin, Preston Brooks, a congressman from South Carolina, beat Sumner so badly with his cane that he almost died. Stevens's and Sumner's commitment and passion made the Radical Republicans a powerful force during and after the war. Even Vice President Andrew Johnson sided with the Radicals on some issues.

Lincoln attempted to bring the Radicals, the moderates, conservatives, and the loyal "war" Democrats into a coalition. Unfortunately, this effort failed. It was not until 1872 that a group called the Liberal Republicans challenged the Radicals. These Republicans advocated for a return to classic republicanism, and even though they garnered Democrat support, their efforts to win the presidency failed.

The power of the Radical Republicans can also be seen in the twenty-one pieces of legislation that Johnson vetoed during his presidency. Out of these twenty-one vetoes, Congress overrode fifteen of them. The Radical Republicans' work also led to ten Republican governments forming in the previous Confederate states.

In 1866, the Radical Republicans took control of Congress due to their opposition to President Johnson's Reconstruction policies. Plenty of violence had resulted from these policies, and it was more than enough for Northern voters to consider voting for a more radical faction. The Memphis riots and the New Orleans riots of 1866 are a few examples of the violence that took place.

When Lincoln proposed the Ten Percent Plan back in 1863, both moderate Republicans and proslavery Democrats, in addition to the Radical Republicans, opposed his Reconstruction plans. In opposition to the Ten Percent Plan, the Radical Republicans passed their own Reconstruction plan, which is known as the Wade-Davis Bill. Lincoln pocket-vetoed their plan in 1864 (meaning he took no action to enact the bill) because it was too harsh.

The Wade-Davis Bill

The Wade-Davis Bill was rather extreme. The Radical Republicans who passed it wanted 50 percent of the seceded state's voters to take a loyalty oath before the state could be readmitted to the Union. Once this happened, then a state convention could be called to create a new state constitution. Every voter had to swear loyalty to the Union if he wanted to vote. Any state reentering the Union had to ban slavery and guarantee protections for the freed people. Although Republicans insisted the bill should include black men's right to vote, the final version did not include that wording. It was all irrelevant in the end anyway due to Lincoln's displeasure with the bill.

Lincoln thought this plan would only prolong the war he was trying to end, which was why he chose not to sign the bill before Congress recessed that year. This pocket veto effectively killed the bill.

Many Radical Republicans wanted equal rights for blacks, including the right to vote. It seems that before Lincoln was assassinated by John Wilkes Booth, he was also leaning in that direction. In his last speech, which he gave on April 11th, 1865, four days before his death, Lincoln hinted that blacks who served in the military should have the right to vote.

Lincoln's vision for the country's reunification never had a chance to be fully put in place, as he died before the war ended. After Lincoln was assassinated, Vice President Andrew Johnson, a Democrat, succeeded to the presidency. Without Lincoln, Congress dissolved into bitter arguments about the Reconstruction with President Johnson.

Chapter 4 – The Thirteenth Amendment

The Thirteenth Amendment

It is not an easy process to amend the Constitution of the United States. It takes a lot of work, a lot of patience, and usually several years. This endeavor is not undertaken lightly, but it seems most politicians were ready for a change in 1865 when the Thirteenth Amendment became an official part of the Constitution.

Lincoln had used his executive powers as commander-in-chief to issue the Emancipation Proclamation. However, there was some concern that once the war was over, the proclamation would have no teeth. A constitutional amendment freeing the slaves was the only way to be sure abolitionism was the law of the land.

As the war winded down, Congress began to look at how to reunite all the states and how the nation could live in harmony afterward. The radical anti-slavery coalitions started to push for a constitutional amendment to make slavery illegal permanently in the country. A bill was introduced to Congress on December 14th, 1863, to create such an amendment. Representatives James Michell Ashley from Ohio and James F. Wilson from Iowa presented the bill to the House of Representatives. In January of 1864, the Senate received its version through a joint resolution submitted by John B. Henderson of Missouri. These different proposals all went to the Senate Judiciary Committee to have their differences resolved. However, the Radical Republicans were not happy with any of these versions. Charles Sumner presented the Senate with their version on February 8th, 1864.

The Radical Republicans' amendment was simple and straightforward. It stated, "All persons are equal before the law, so that no person can hold another as a slave; and the Congress shall have power to make all laws necessary and proper to carry this declaration into effect everywhere in the United States."

Sumner tried to avoid the Judiciary Committee for consideration of his amendment, as he wanted his own committee to take a look at it, but the Senate sent it there anyway. The Senate Judiciary Committee did not take this version into consideration as they did with the others. Instead, they submitted a version to the Senate based on Wilson's, Ashley's, and Henderson's works.

The Thirteenth Amendment is short and direct. It contains two sections, which you can read below:

Section 1

"Neither slavery nor involuntary servitude, except as a punishment for crime whereof the party shall have been duly convicted, shall exist within the United States, or any place subject to their jurisdiction."

Section 2

"The Congress shall have power to enforce this article by appropriate legislation."

The Senate Judiciary Committee mainly based their draft on Henderson's version, but they did not agree with his stipulation that a constitutional amendment could only be adopted by a majority vote in the House and Senate and ratification by two-thirds of the state legislatures. The rule at the time was two-thirds of each House of Congress and three-fourths of the states.

At the Senate vote on April 8th, 1864, the measure passed. The House had more trouble agreeing. The Democrats, who opposed the amendment, relied on the arguments of states' rights and federalism. Some believed the amendment signaled revolution as opposed to just being a constitutional amendment. These Democrats thought the amendment went against the spirit of the Constitution, while others argued that it would lead to full citizenship for black people. On the other side, Republicans argued that slavery was immoral and uncivilized. They believed that white people were injured by slavery as well. After all, employment rates in the slave states were much lower than in the North due to slave labor. Soon, many Northern Democrats came to support the amendment.

Following his re-election, Lincoln threw his administration's power behind the amendment. He made it the top priority of his second term. Members of his administration plied Democrats with promises of campaign contributions or positions in the government. When the House appeared to be only a handful of votes from passing the second vote, Lincoln went all out to secure its passage. The amendment passed the House on January 31st, 1865.

On February 1st, 1865, the amendment was sent to the states to be ratified. At that time, there were thirty-six states in the Union, including those states that had seceded. Out of that number, twenty-seven states would have to ratify the amendment for it to become the law of the land. In less than thirty days, eighteen states had already ratified it. Most of the Northern states ratified the amendment very quickly, as did most of the loyal border states. However, they didn't pass it quickly enough for Lincoln to see the nation freed. The final approval of the amendment was due to the Johnson administration's work in currying the favor of North Carolina, Alabama, and Georgia. By gaining their accession, the amendment had the required number of twenty-seven states, and the amendment became a part of the United States Constitution before the end of the year.

The Effectiveness of the Thirteenth Amendment

Once the amendment was ratified, celebration broke out, especially among the Radical Republicans and the black population. There were both immediate and long-term ramifications of this action. To review some of the most significant impacts:

- The system of chattel slavery that existed before the war was made illegal.
- In Kentucky, between 65,000 and 100,000 slaves were freed immediately.
- In Delaware, around 900 individuals immediately became freed people.
- The Fugitive Slave Clause was nullified, as was the Three-Fifths Compromise. The Three-Fifths Compromise was added to the US Constitution in 1787, and it gave a boost to the Southern states, which were not as populous as the North. According to the compromise, every three out of five slaves would be counted as people. With the passage of the Thirteenth Amendment, former slaves would all count for demographic reasons and to increase Congress's apportionment in the South.
- Millions of slaves were freed, but they had no way of supporting themselves or their families. They had no land and no opportunities except to stay on the plantations and work for low wages. However, even though they were earning money now, they were no longer sheltered and fed by the plantation owners.
- All the slaves had been freed without appropriate protections or legal status. Some historians believe they were treated even worse than they had been as slaves, as there were no protections in place.

- Laws were passed in the South to criminalize as many blacks as possible. These were called the Black Codes.
- The Thirteenth Amendment allowed for the punishment of forced labor for those convicted of a crime. The Northwest Ordinance of 1787 included the same type of wording, as Congress had simply lifted it and added it to the amendment. There was no consideration of the ramifications of this clause. This clause is still a part of the amendment, although current legislators are attempting to change it.

The Thirteenth Amendment certainly ended chattel slavery. However, it didn't necessarily make the lives of freed people much easier. Slavery could still be used as a punishment for crime, and laws, known as the Black Codes, were designed to essentially trap black people into committing crimes. For instance, blacks could be sentenced to forced labor for selling cotton after sunset or not contracting with a white farmer; if they refused to sign the contract, they would be considered vagrants. Freed people were subjected to violence, white supremacy, and the inconsistent enforcement of laws. Of course, most of this took place in the South, but the North was not blameless.

This clause resulted in many ex-slaves being imprisoned on old plantations and being subjected to involuntary labor. The prisoners saw the guards at these sites as just another overseer. The Virginia Supreme Court even justified this treatment in 1871. In this ruling, the court declared the prisoners to be slaves of the state.

So, regardless of the designers' intentions, this amendment did not confer any civil rights on the black population, and they faced an uphill battle. The Reconstruction policies should have helped alleviate the problem, but as you will discover in the following pages, they didn't go far enough.

Judicial Reviews of the Thirteenth Amendment

The Thirteenth Amendment brought a lot of change to the nation, and as a result, it was questioned time and time again or used to support a ruling. The first time a high-level court was asked to look at the Thirteenth Amendment was in 1866. Here is a brief overview of some of the cases.

1866 – *United States v. Rhodes* concerned black people's ability to get redress in the federal courts. In this case, Kentucky had a law that did not allow blacks to testify against whites. The lawsuit specifically involved a black woman who was robbed by a white man. Since the woman was unable to testify against the man, it prevented her from attaining justice.

The Kentucky Supreme Court ruled that the woman could not appeal to the federal courts for redress. However, a Supreme Court justice overruled the Kentucky decision based on the Civil Rights Act of 1866, which set the foundation for black citizenship in the US.

1872 – In *Blyew v. United States,* two white men were visiting the cabin of a black family. John Blyew became angry and hit one of the sons on the head with an ax twice. The two men then killed his parents and grandmother. They also seriously wounded two of the younger children.

The Supreme Court ruled that the children didn't have a case because only living people could take advantage of the Civil Rights Act. In other words, this meant the Thirteenth Amendment did not provide any relief in murder cases. Not all the justices agreed with this ruling, saying that the Thirteenth Amendment needed to be interpreted in a way that would give black people some standing in society. However, they were in the minority. This case set a precedent and led to the Thirteenth Amendment's loss of power.

1896 – The attorneys in the case of *Plessy v. Ferguson* used the Thirteenth Amendment to argue against racial segregation. They argued that because of segregation, there were "observances of a servile character coincident with the incidents of slavery," which was in violation of the Thirteenth Amendment. The lawyers argued that the "distinction between race and caste" violated the Constitution. Unfortunately, the Supreme Court didn't agree, saying that it could not eliminate social legalities and distinctions that were based on color. It was up to the state to decide which laws to pass and if they were reasonable enough. This was the famous "separate but equal" decision.

1906 – In *Hodges v. United States*, the Supreme Court again used the Thirteenth Amendment, this time to prevent justice for those who conspired to commit violence. A group of white men used violent means to prevent a group of black men from working. The white men were convicted in Kentucky of a conspiracy to deprive citizens of their liberty. However, the US Supreme Court ruled that violent assault or aggression did not "reduce the individual to a condition of slavery." Therefore, they declared the Kentucky ruling to be unconstitutional.

1911 – In *Bailey v. Alabama*, the Supreme Court ruled that the Thirteenth Amendment covered more than just chattel slavery. The court ruled that "The plain intention [of the amendment] was to abolish slavery of whatever name and form and all its badges and incidents; to render impossible any state of bondage; to make labor free, by prohibiting that control by which the personal service of one man is disposed of or coerced for another's benefit, which is the essence of involuntary servitude."

1968 – *Jones v. Alfred H. Mayer Co.* is an interesting example of how far the interpretation of the Thirteenth Amendment had stretched by the 20ᵗʰ century. The Jones family sued the Alfred H. Mayer real estate company for not selling them a home. The Supreme Court ruled that Congress may act "to prevent private actors from imposing badges and incidents of servitude." Congress had the authority under the Thirteenth Amendment to decide what those "badges and incidents of servitude" were. The Supreme Court also upheld the Civil Rights Act of 1866, saying that it prohibited private and state-backed discrimination.

There were many other cases that involved the Thirteenth Amendment. Some of the more recent ones include when the US Supreme Court ruled that the military draft did not equate to involuntary servitude during the Vietnam War or when the US Court of Appeals ruled that schools imposing community service as a condition of high school graduation did not engage in involuntary servitude.

Although the Thirteenth Amendment still has ramifications for today's society, back in the 1860s, people feared what the effects of the amendment might mean for the nation. President Andrew Johnson fully approved of the Thirteenth Amendment, but he tried to placate some of those fears, especially for those living in the South, during his Reconstruction efforts.

Chapter 5 – Presidential Reconstruction

Most historians believe that if Lincoln had lived, the Reconstruction would have been drastically different. For one, there would have been a substantial federal role in overseeing the entire Reconstruction era. Andrew Johnson did not think the federal government should play a major role in this at all. But Johnson was a Democrat, and having more power in the federal government instead of the states' hands went against their beliefs.

Following the passage of the Thirteenth Amendment, Congress was in recess. President Andrew Johnson decided this was a good time for him to design his own Reconstruction plan. This period is known as the "Presidential Reconstruction." During this time, President Johnson oversaw the new Southern governments and the states' political conventions as they reentered the Union. Johnson chose the delegates to these conventions based on their loyalty to him.

Johnson would not demand much from the Confederate states rejoining the Union. Three major issues faced each state in their conventions to become a part of the nation again. These issues were the secession, the abolition of slavery, and resolving the war debt.

Once the states reunited with the Union, Johnson believed the Southern states should then take control of their own government and Reconstruction efforts.

The first conventions, which were held in 1865, took place in North Carolina, Alabama, South Carolina, Florida, Mississippi, and Georgia. Johnson wanted the Thirteenth Amendment ratified by all the Southern states before Congress reconvened that December. He knew he would be in a fight over the Reconstruction efforts with the Radical Republicans, and he wanted the leverage the South could bring him. If he ratified the Thirteenth Amendment, freeing the slaves in the process, Johnson would be able to point to the willingness of the Southern states to change and embrace a new way of life. By doing this, Johnson would show the American public that it would be wrong to let the Southern states stay out of the Union while also demonstrating the South's ability to make the right decisions on their own, without major interference from the federal government.

However, to do this, Johnson had to negotiate with the Southern states, offering them a vision of how they could enact the amendment. Johnson certainly wanted freed people to enjoy some rights, but he went so far as to promise Southern governors that they would control how they gave out rights to the freed slaves. This would have allowed the white supremacists in the South to have a large role in how the Reconstruction proceeded. In time, they made it incredibly difficult for blacks to hold office or even vote. They also demanded that the freed slaves return any land that the federal government had granted them under the "forty acres and a mule" order. This land went back to the former slave owners, leaving the blacks with no land and no money.

The promise of "forty acres and a mule" had been made by Union General William Tecumseh Sherman. General Sherman had land in Florida, Georgia, and South Carolina reserved for the resettlement of the freed slaves. If a freed slave took an oath of loyalty to the Union, they were eligible to settle on and lease up to forty acres of land. He also planned for there to be an option to purchase the land in a few years. Sadly, this promise was an empty one due to President Johnson's administration. Although some black people were able to take advantage of it, it never happened in the way that Sherman had planned.

Even though Johnson did his best to placate the South over the Thirteenth Amendment, the wording of it did not please all the Southern politicians. The Southern governments were afraid the North would use the enforcement clause (the one that states Congress has the power to pass legislation to support the amendment) to impose blacks suffrage everywhere in the Union. Several Southern states ratified the amendment with stipulations that Congress could not legislate policy that went against the Constitution in regards to the former slaves.

President Johnson's basic attitude was one of laissez-faire and strong state governments. Unlike the Radical Republicans, he favored states' rights and a less powerful central government. He believed the federal government had no business interfering in the economy and social life of the states, which led him to oppose legislation that impacted the economy in any way.

In an attempt to keep the Radical Republicans from challenging his plans, Johnson declared the end of Reconstruction before Congress even reconvened in 1865. Congress was furious, and when the members reconvened, they passed a series of bills, some of which Johnson vetoed. He objected to reorganizing the economy of the South or dismantling the plantation system, and he did not hold many strong beliefs in regards to protecting the civil rights of the freed slaves. While he expected the blacks to have some rights, Johnson did not believe that blacks should have the same rights as the white population, routinely calling black people inferior.

Needless to say, Johnson's legacy is a bit mixed. Some scholars believe he tried his best to carry out Lincoln's vision, even though he didn't agree with all of his policies. He refused to bend to Congress's whim, a Congress that consistently voted against his vetoes, and he worked on a plan that adhered strictly to the Constitution. This plan ultimately failed, and Congress essentially took the reins from him. But even Johnson's supporters realize that he wasn't a strong leader. He certainly was not the best person to oversee the Reconstruction. He also wasn't as committed to the Reconstruction efforts as other leaders, such as Lincoln, would have been, and he wasn't a man that compromised, which affected the freed slaves most of all, as they did not have a good footing in society.

Chapter 6 – The Civil Rights Act of 1866

The Joint Committee on Reconstruction, 1865

When the Radical Republicans came back into session in December of 1865, they found that President Johnson had conducted and completed his Reconstruction plan. They also discovered that he had pardoned many influential and high-ranking Southerners and let them keep their lands. In their eyes, this Reconstruction was too soft on the South. The Radicals knew Johnson's Reconstruction efforts were even worse than what Lincoln had planned.

The Radical Republicans knew they had to do something. Not only were they angered by Johnson's actions, but they also felt disrespected. The Republicans were greatly concerned that Johnson's Reconstruction held no security for the freed slaves and that instead of helping those who had just escaped bondage, the president chose to appease Southern plantation owners who had left the Union.

To combat these actions, Congress established the Joint Committee on Reconstruction in late 1865 to establish its own plan. This coalition, which included three Democrats, gave the Radicals enough power to put the Reconstruction in the hands of Congress. This led to veto after veto from Johnson, although Congress was able to override most of them. Johnson's attempt to create a coalition of moderates failed to overcome the power of the Radicals, who were able to legislate their plan for Reconstruction.

This plan began with the Civil Rights Act of 1866.

In 1865 and 1866, many of the former Confederate states passed legislation known as the Black Codes. These will be discussed in more depth later on, but for now, it is important to understand that these codes were meant to keep freed slaves from going where or doing what they wanted. Their goal was to keep the freed people as a source of labor in the South.

The Black Codes were the forerunners of the infamous Jim Crow laws, and they enraged the Radical Republicans and the abolitionists of the North. Congress's first response was to refuse to allow any senator or congress member from the South to be seated in the new Congress. While they were unable to keep Southern representatives out of the government, the Radical Republicans did have an overwhelming majority in both Houses of Congress by 1866. In the first half of 1866, the Republicans got to work and passed two major pieces of legislation. These were the Civil Rights Act of 1866 and the Freedmen's Bureau Act.

The Civil Rights Act of 1866

As Southern states pushed the limits with the Black Codes, Radical Republicans needed a way to push back. That way was the Civil Rights Act of 1866.

In general, the law defined citizenship and affirmed that all citizens were equal under the law. This act aimed to protect the rights and citizenship of those who had African descent and were born in the United States.

By utilizing the power Congress had given itself in the Thirteenth Amendment, Senator Lyman Trumbull authored a bill that would actually benefit black people. Trumbull is also notable for his work on the Thirteenth Amendment. Congress passed the act on April 9th, 1886, but it was not ratified until 1870. To begin with, Johnson vetoed the act two separate times, once in 1865 and again in 1866. There was a general belief among politicians (not just Johnson) that Congress could not give itself the power to define citizenship. There needed to be a constitutional amendment for that. However, there was a two-thirds majority in both the House and Senate that supported the act, and they easily overrode the presidential veto the second time around.

The Civil Rights Act of 1866 is quite long, but we will take a closer look at the most important parts.

Section One of the Civil Rights Act

This is the most important part of the bill, as it bestows upon all people born in the United States, besides the Native Americans, the right to citizenship. It grants these citizens "of every race and color, without regard to any previous condition of slavery or involuntary servitude, except as a punishment for a crime whereof the party shall have been duly convicted" the "same right in every State and Territory to make and enforce contracts, to sue, be parties, give evidence, and to the full and equal benefit of all laws and proceedings for the security of persons and property as is enjoyed by white citizens, and shall be subject to like punishment, pains, penalties, taxes, licenses, and exactions of every kind, and to no other."

Just this opening section was anathema to the members of the former Confederate States of America, as black people who had been born into slavery in the United States had automatic citizenship. Given that President Johnson's sympathies lay with the South, this first section alone gave him enough ammunition to veto the bill. What Southerner would agree that former slaves and freemen had the right to enter into contracts and sue anyone in court? What Southerner would agree that former slaves and freemen could testify in court or buy, sell, or inherit property? What former Confederate would concur that these former slaves and freemen should enjoy the same laws as they did? These were the kind of ideas and laws that had started the Civil War in the first place. Johnson wanted to reunite the Union without upsetting the South more than they already were. On top of that, this bill certainly did not fall in line with Johnson's Reconstruction plans.

You might have noticed that the Civil Rights Act did not extend to Native Americans. In actuality, it extended to those Native Americans who paid federal taxes, but there were very few of them. Most Native Americans at this time either lived on reservations or in unsettled territories. Since they did not pay federal taxes and were subject to their own reservation governments, the US government did not include them in census counts. In other words, they had no voice in Congress, so no one fought for their rights on the bigger stage of US politics. Native Americans became US citizens in 1924, but like African Americans, they had to jump through many hurdles before their voice could finally be heard, a struggle that is still ongoing today.

Section Two

This section didn't sit any better with the Southerners. The Civil Rights Act went on to state that anyone who went against this act—in other words, anyone who sought to curtail the liberties of another person as stated in the above section, regardless of their skin color— "shall be deemed guilty of a misdemeanor, and, on conviction shall be punished by fine not exceeding one thousand dollars, or imprisonment not exceeding one year, or both, in the discretion of the court."

Not only were the Northern Republicans in Congress saying that ex-slaves had the same rights as white Southerners, but they were also saying whites could go to jail if they didn't honor those rights. If you had been a son of the Confederacy, it would have only taken one quick read of this legislation to send you into a boiling rage. And we're not even halfway through the act.

Section Three

This is a rather lengthy section, but it really comes down to these words. "The jurisdiction in civil and criminal matters hereby conferred on the district and circuit courts of the United States shall be exercised and enforced in conformity with the laws of the United States, so far as such laws are suitable to carry the same into effect."

In other words, if a person of color cannot get a fair trial in the state courts, the federal district and circuit courts will have jurisdiction.

Section Four

This section talked about what would happen if someone violated this act. It states that "the district attorneys, marshals, and deputy marshals of the United States...and every other officer who may be specially empowered by the President of the United States, shall be, and they are hereby, specially authorized and required...to institute proceedings against all and every person who shall violate the provisions of this act and cause him or them to be arrested and imprisoned, or bailed, as the case may be, for trial before such court of the United States."

Highlights of the Other Sections

There were ten sections in all. While the first four are the most pertinent to the discussion of Reconstruction, there are notable parts in the other sections. For instance, section five gives the United States military the power to enforce the non-slavery clause. Section eight provides the president with the right to have the military take action if he has "reason to believe that offences have been or are likely to be committed against the provisions of this act." Finally, the act ends with the US Supreme Court having the final say over any issues arising from this act.

That is a lot to take in, but the bottom line is that it was good for those freed by the Thirteenth Amendment. However, the former Confederates, in addition to other Southerners as well as people in the North, didn't see the Civil Rights Act in such a positive light. The question was raised as to whether Congress had the constitutional authority to enact this law, and as a result of these discussions, it was not even ratified until after the Fourteenth Amendment, which defined US citizenship, was passed.

Truthfully, the act seems more impactful than it actually turned out to be. Under constant pressure from Democrats, a significant part of the act was deleted. This had stated, "there shall be no discrimination in civil rights or immunities among the inhabitants of any State or Territory of the United States on account of race, color, or previous condition of servitude." Congress could not lay out what they meant by "civil rights," and even Republicans were worried that the courts might interpret the term too broadly. It is also important to note that the Civil Rights Act of 1866 did not grant black men the right to vote.

The act contained much of the same language as the Fourteenth Amendment, including equality before the law. The same type of language can also be found in the Second Freedmen's Bureau Act of 1866. With all this repetition, it was evident where Congress, which was led by the Republicans, stood on slavery and civil rights for blacks.

Some sections of this law are still enforceable today, particularly the section granting every citizen the right to enter into contracts, to sue, to testify against another in court, and the security of a person's property.

It was not until the 20th century that the Supreme Court validated Trumbull's contention that the Thirteenth Amendment gave Congress the right to legislate on these matters. In fact, it was due to the question of how much authority Congress had that the Fourteenth Amendment was drawn up. This amendment enshrined the major provisions of the Civil Rights Act of 1866 so that no future Congress could change them.

But how did the act fare in the face of Southern defiance? It was not as successful as the Radical Republicans hoped it would be. The activities of the Ku Klux Klan negatively affected its implementation. Discrimination in housing and employment was effectively illegal according to this legislation, but that was not the reality. These issues were still being litigated in the 20th century.

Freedmen's Bureau

A vital part of the Radical Republicans' Reconstruction plan was the Freedmen's Bureau, which was created by Congress in 1865. This organization's goal was to assist former slaves through the Reconstruction era. The Freedmen's Bureau was designed to establish schools, distribute confiscated property, and provide food and supplies.

Lincoln was around when the Freedmen's Bureau Bill was passed, although he died a little over a month later. Since it was created during the war, the Freedmen's Bureau operated under the auspices of the United States Department of War. In the beginning, most of the workers at the Bureau were Union soldiers. During this time, Congress did not allocate funds or hire knowledgeable personnel to make the Freedmen's Bureau effective.

As one might expect, Southerners and ex-Confederates did not welcome the Bureau. Southerners who had lost land during the war fully expected to get it back. This was especially true because Lincoln and Johnson allowed high-level Confederate officials to keep their land. The more affluent people in the South were not intimidated by the Bureau and thwarted its effectiveness. It also didn't help that the Bureau's staff were poor soldiers who often ignored the Southern abuse of former slaves for a small payoff. The Bureau also faced strong opposition from President Johnson. Johnson believed that the federal government should not play a role in protecting the former slaves or interfering with the states' judicial systems.

Despite these issues, the Freedmen's Bureau still managed to do some good. It helped to resettle thousands of war refugees and built schools. By the end of 1865, more than 90,000 former slaves were enrolled in public schools.

Congress introduced and passed a new Freedmen's Bureau bill in 1866, adding special federal courts that could overrule the Southern state courts. However, President Johnson vetoed this bill. Congress worked hard on attaining a new bill that would please everyone, introducing a new one later that year. But yet again, Johnson vetoed it. This time around, Congress was able to agree, and they overrode the veto, which greatly displeased the president. In 1868, Congress tried to extend the Freedmen's Bureau, but they decided not to go ahead with the vote. Four years later, the Freedmen's Bureau closed.

In the seven years the Bureau was in operation, it had impressive success, even though it failed to accomplish all it had intended. The Freedmen's Bureau was set up into districts across the rebel states. Bureau personnel were spread out across the South, and usually, they were the only federal representatives in the area. They faced harassment, threats, violence, and ridicule.

The Bureau provided food for millions (including poor whites, although there was more of an emphasis on assisting the freed slaves), built schools and hospitals, and negotiated labor contracts for blacks. They also helped blacks find their family members from whom they had been separated.

Perhaps the Freedmen's Bureau's most significant accomplishment was establishing schools and universities. Before the Bureau, the South had no education system in place for blacks, and it is unlikely they would have created a state-sponsored education for the freed slaves, at least right away. Howard University owes its existence to the Bureau. The Freedmen's Bureau was also instrumental in establishing Hampton University in Virginia and Fisk University in Tennessee.

However, there were many shortcomings, and much of it had to do with the state of the South after the war. Since much of the infrastructure had been destroyed, the Bureau had to start from scratch. Racism was still prevalent, with white Southern doctors refusing to treat black people, which led to the spread of disease. In addition to this, members of the Bureau were regularly harassed and blocked from assisting where they were needed.

In March 1872, the commissioner of the Bureau was asked to head West to deal with the Native Americans. While he was gone, the Bureau steadily went under. The North was no longer invested in keeping the Bureau afloat. The South was still violent toward the Bureau's members, and it didn't seem to be getting any better as the years went by. In addition, by 1871, the South had formed constitutions that established universal public education, showing some progress when it came to equal rights. When the commissioner returned from the West that November, he found that the Bureau no longer existed.

Black Codes

Throughout the Reconstruction era, the South established something known as the Black Codes. These were the forerunners of the Jim Crow laws and were backed by a young Ku Klux Klan.

According to Southern politicians, the Black Codes were supposed to help revitalize the Southern economy. To be fair, the Southern economy was in dire straits. The war had done a lot of damage, and in addition to that, the slave labor force that the cotton and tobacco plantations had depended on had suddenly disappeared. As a result, the Black Codes were put in place so the blacks could still be used as a dependable labor force. However, many in the South saw this as the freed slaves' rightful place—a source of labor and nothing more. Southerners saw blacks who were not working as vagrants, which was punishable by the Black

Codes. Freed people no longer wanted to work back-breaking hours; they wanted time to rest and enjoy themselves too, but many whites viewed this as laziness. Their racist views of African Americans permeated these codes, and in some cases, states just used the same wording they had used in the slave codes, this time using the word "Negro" instead of "slave."

Life in the South was very hard for the freed slaves. Besides the abuses they would receive because of their skin color, many could not find work. As a result, many of them became sharecroppers for white plantation owners. Sharecroppers were either black or poor white tenant farmers who rented their land from wealthy landowners. In essence, this is a form of slavery, and for many, their situation was not much better than it had been before the war. Other Black Codes made it criminal to be unemployed, in debt, vote, or have sex with a white woman. These codes legalized racism, giving birth to systemic racism in the United States, something which African Americans struggle with to this day. Using these codes as an excuse, the Ku Klux Klan terrorized blacks all across the South and Midwest. If a black person was arrested under these codes, they could be sentenced to forced labor, as it had been approved by the Thirteenth Amendment.

So regardless of the Thirteenth Amendment and the Civil Rights Act, blacks in the South essentially had no civil rights and lived in poverty. Some historians believe that many were worse off than when they were slaves.

The North was not blameless either. Some Northern politicians agreed with the reasoning behind the Black Codes, and some states even passed their own Black Codes. Indiana, Illinois, and Michigan all passed laws that banned the marriage of white and black people, something that all the Southern states had in place. Some Northern states had the same vagrancy laws as the South did, as well as laws that made black orphans available for whites to hire as a labor source. There was segregation, and for the most part, blacks were not able to vote.

In a large portion of the North and almost all of the South, the belief in white supremacy was embedded in the culture. In addition, many in the South took out their postwar anger on black people. The fact that blacks could be arrested for just being in a certain place (vagrancy) and forced into working for the whites led to a system of convict leasing. As this became more prominent, the South realized that it was more profitable to arrest black men and force them into labor. These men were essentially still slaves, just by a different name.

Chapter 7 – The Radical Reconstruction

The Reconstruction Act of 1867

In 1866, Northern voters reacted to the Presidential Reconstruction by voting in an overwhelmingly Radical Republican Congress. Given this increased power, Congress wrested the Reconstruction policies from the president.

Radical Reconstruction was also called Congressional Reconstruction, and it looked nothing like Johnson's Presidential Reconstruction. The Radical Republicans were determined to undo the lenient actions of President Johnson, and since they held enough control in both Houses of Congress to override any of Johnson's vetoes, they got to work. In March 1867, Congress passed the First Reconstruction Act of 1867.

In this act, the Confederate states were divided into military districts. It laid out how the Southern states would be governed, despite Johnson's earlier state conventions and reinstatements. Universal male suffrage was to be the law, and Confederate states would have to ratify the Fourteenth Amendment with all of its clauses intact, even though it infuriated the South. The Fourteenth Amendment was not a new bill; Congress had sent this amendment to the states for ratification in 1866 (it will be talked about in more detail in a separate chapter). Each state reentering the Union would also have state constitutions that mirrored the Thirteenth and Fourteenth Amendments. The Radical Republicans asserted the rights of black freedmen throughout the country, but especially in the South. In this environment, blacks would begin to participate in public life.

You can imagine the response of the ex-Confederates at this demand. After President Lincoln's and President Johnson's cooperative Reconstruction effort, this treatment must have come as a shock. It was demoralizing and depressing for white Southerners. And adding insult to injury, Congress demanded that each Confederate state ratify the Fourteenth Amendment, which clarified citizenship and the rights of citizens, and allow blacks to vote if they wanted to be part of the Union.

Many of these states had already agreed to Johnson's terms for reinstatement, and now they had to start all over again and rewrite their state constitution. This time around, they needed to incorporate the basic ideas of the Thirteenth and Fourteenth Amendments. The occupying Union troops were to oversee the voter registration of non-white men to ensure they had the right to vote.

When the Radical Republican Congress looked at the riots in New Orleans and Memphis, they determined that the Reconstruction was not harsh enough. Memphis saw its people turn against each other in May 1866. A large group of African Americans, mainly former veterans, gathered together and refused to disperse when asked by the police. Tensions escalated until two police officers had been shot. This incited a riot, with an angry mob of whites attacking blacks and burning down homes, schools, and churches. It is believed that forty-six African Americans and two European Americans died in the chaos. The New Orleans riots took place in late July of the same year. Black freedmen engaged in a peaceful demonstration, which was beset by white rioters. Between 30 and 50 blacks died, with around 150 wounded. It is believed that three whites also perished. Rather than see the riots as a message that Johnson's Reconstruction was too punitive, Congress pressed ahead, determined to enforce its will upon the South.

Although the white Southerners did not care for the Radical Reconstruction, the ex-slaves and the black community in general advanced somewhat. It was a much better situation than what Andrew Johnson's Presidential Reconstruction would have been. Still, it was not all positive. The white Southerners' strong and violent reactions greatly impacted the lives of black Southerners. For the most part, white Southerners ignored the laws that had been passed by Congress that granted rights to the ex-slaves. For African Americans, as well as the poor whites in the South, not much changed.

However, for a short time, the South experienced large scale interracial democracy. Black men could vote and run for office, winning seats in local and state governments and then winning seats on a federal level in Congress. This was due to the hidden agenda of the Republicans, which was to create a political stronghold in the South. By 1870, all the Confederate states had reunited with the Union, and the Republicans ran most of the state governments. Republican carpetbaggers, scalawags, and blacks made up the southern Republican Party, but by the end of the 1870s, the control was back in the hands of the Democrats. Jim Crow laws, poll taxes, the Ku Klux Klan, and many other factors would help to strip the blacks' rights away once again. However, in the beginning, there was a lot of advancement for blacks, especially in government.

It might be astonishing to some readers to hear how many blacks served in government during the Radical Reconstruction. More than 600 blacks served in state and local offices. The local offices they held were anything from the sheriff to the justice of the peace. And at least sixteen blacks served in the United States Congress. With blacks serving in local and state governments, public schools were established, laborers on plantations gained more bargaining power, and taxes were made more equitable. Racial discrimination in accommodations and public transportation was made illegal. The federal government supported the South with funding for railroads and new businesses. This was all good for the ex-slaves, but white Southerners felt more alienated and angrier with each passing day.

Chapter 8 – Carpetbaggers and Scallywags, 1867

After the Civil War came to a close, whites and, to an extent, blacks began to migrate south to promote the ideals the Radical Republicans were touting in Congress. In addition to them, there were also white Southerners who supported these efforts. These groups would come together to govern the South during the Radical Reconstruction. These governments were responsible for setting up charities, building schools, and improving infrastructure, namely shipping lanes and railroad transportation.

The people who came from the North were called carpetbaggers, regardless of race, while the white Southerners who supported the Radical Reconstruction were called scallywags. You might be wondering what is with the odd names. There was a lot of resentment among native white Southerners of every class toward the Northerners, who were essentially coming down to govern them. They were also angry at their own people for turning against them for an opportunity to advance further in government.

Following the Reconstruction Act of 1867, Southern governments were replaced by the Union military until new elections could be held. Freed slaves and freemen were able to vote and run in these elections. Those who held high positions in the Confederate government or military were stripped of their right to vote and hold office. These restrictions were later rescinded when all the Confederate states reentered the Union.

Due to these changes, blacks made up an overwhelming majority in the Republican Party of the South. Together with the Northern carpetbaggers and Southern scallywags, they were able to control most of the Southern legislatures and executive branches. Thus, whites and blacks governed together for the first time in the South.

Carpetbaggers

Who exactly were the carpetbaggers, and why did most Southerners resent or even hate their presence? The word "carpetbagger" gets its meaning from roaming individuals who arrive in a place they do not come from with only a carpetbag or satchel. Some opportunistic Northerners saw a chance after the war to move to the South and make their fortunes. White Southerners saw these people as outsiders and scoundrels, as they believed they were coming to exploit the people, whether it was in regards to money, land, or politics.

Carpetbaggers came to the South intending to buy land, partner with plantation owners who had no resources, or lease plantations. The carpetbaggers saw cotton as a way of making their fortune. After all, someone had to run the plantations and keep the economy going. However, to the established Southerner, the carpetbaggers were ruthless, opportunistic, lower-class whites who sought to make a fortune off their broken backs. There was tremendous resentment and scorn toward these Northerners as a result.

The truth was these Northerners were actually often middle class and well educated. They brought tremendous knowledge and resources to the South. They were businessmen, teachers, journalists, and merchants. Some were even with the Freedman's Bureau, and many had been soldiers in the Union Army. They considered themselves to be reformers who wanted to help build a new South in the model image of the North.

Scalawags

When the first Radical Reconstruction legislatures were set up in the South after the war, they were filled with white Southern Republicans. The Democrats referred to them as scalawags. It can also be spelled scallywag. The term is as old as the 1840s, and it refers to a farm animal that has no value but is taking up resources. Southerners used it to mean a worthless person, and this was exactly how white Southerners saw their fellow Southerners who assisted or were loyal to the Union. In the white Southerners' eyes, a scalawag was much worse than a carpetbagger because they were from the South. Many considered them to be traitors.

Many scalawags were plantation owners or closeted abolitionists. They believed in black civil rights but also wanted to retain white control over the economy and political structures. Many of these Southern Republicans had been members of the Whig Party, which had fallen apart in 1854.

These Southerners believed they were better off joining the Republicans than being in opposition, as most of the South was. This group made up about 20 percent of the white voters in the South, and they came to hold a good deal of power in the local legislatures. Some had served in Congress or had been judges before the war.

The Radical Reconstruction

While Northerners were angry over Johnson's Presidential Reconstruction, many Southerners were mad at the Republicans for the Radical Reconstruction, as the Radical Reconstruction intended to undo what the Johnson Reconstruction had planned.

The Radical Reconstruction was based on the Republicans' view of freedom and equal rights, but Southerners hung on to their old worldview of slavery and free labor. As a result of their beliefs, the carpetbaggers and scallywags were easy scapegoats. They were labeled as scum and demeaned as being on the same level as the blacks. The Southern Democrats later used this rhetoric to rally the old South after the Republicans were defeated in 1877.

An editor of an Alabama paper defined the Reconstruction era scalawags, saying, "Our scalawag is the local leper of the community. Unlike the carpetbagger, he is native, which is so much worse. Once he was respected in his circle...and he could look his neighbor in the face. Now, possessed of the itch of office and the salt rheum of Radicalism, he is a mangy dog, slinking through the alleys, haunting the Governor's office, defiling with tobacco juice the steps of the Capitol, stretching his lazy carcass in the sun on the Square, or the benches of the Mayor's court." This viewpoint was quite prevalent, and it is easy to see how the scalawag came to be the hated symbol of the Radical Reconstruction.

Let's look beyond the stereotypes, though, and see what good these men created in the South. During the war, Union troops occupied the city of New Orleans. Once the war was over, there were still tens of thousands of Unionists in the city, including soldiers, planter lessees, and treasury agents. Many of these people stayed in New Orleans after the war, and they were seen as carpetbaggers by white Southerners. The first two governors after the Radical Reconstruction began were people that fell into this category. So were the three senators that Louisiana sent to Washington, DC, along with ten representatives. Oftentimes, the Speaker of the Louisiana House was a "carpetbagger."

These men had the knowledge and experience to run the newly configured state government. They ran the Post Office, the Internal Revenue Service, the Mint, the Customs House, the State Land Office, and the Fifth Circuit Federal Court. At the same time, Southern Democrats owned most of the land and ran most of the businesses, and the Ku Klux Klan targeted both scalawags and carpetbaggers.

Chapter 9 – The Fourteenth Amendment, 1868

Three years after the Thirteenth Amendment was ratified and two years after the Civil Rights Bill was passed, Congress was sitting on several pieces of legislation. One of them was an integral amendment of the US Constitution: the Fourteenth Amendment.

There are five sections to the Fourteenth Amendment. This amendment was often called the Reconstruction Amendment, and it gave us such familiar phrases as "due process" and "equal protection under the law."

It also cleared up the issue of representation to Congress. In the Constitution, slaves counted as three-fifths of a person. In the Thirteenth Amendment, ex-slaves became one person. Yet Congress still felt the need to add this clause to the Fourteenth Amendment: "Representation shall be apportioned among the several states according to the respective numbers, counting the whole number of persons in each state, excluding Indians not taxed." Representation to Congress continues to be apportioned in this manner today.

Let's take a look at the clauses of the Fourteenth Amendment in closer detail. It certainly starts off with a bang. "All persons born or naturalized in the United States...are citizens of the United States and of the State wherein they reside." With these words, Congress made it clear that ex-slaves and their children were automatically citizens of the United States. If they had been born in Africa, there was a process for becoming a naturalized citizen.

This section goes on to say, "No State shall make or enforce any law which shall abridge the privileges and immunities of citizens." But what exactly were those privileges? It hearkens back to a phrase most Americans are familiar with today—life, liberty, and property. Sounds pretty familiar to the words set down by the Founding Fathers almost 100 years before. The Fourteenth Amendment also stated that citizens should not be deprived of the "due process of law; nor deny to any person within its jurisdiction the equal protection of the laws."

The keywords here are "due process of law" and "equal protection of the laws." In fact, they might be the most important phrases in the amendment. In all the years since the Civil War, Americans have hung their liberty on the Due Process Clause and the Equal Protection Clause. Many Americans take these rights for granted today, but they were bombshells to the American people back in the late 1800s.

The next section of the Fourteenth Amendment covers the allocation of representatives; as mentioned above, the Three-Fifths Compromise was no longer in effect, and everyone counted as one person (excluding Native Americans). But more importantly, this section gave all black men the right to vote in the country.

> But when the right to vote at any election...is denied to any of the male inhabitants of such State, being twenty-one years of age, and citizens of the United States, or in any way abridged, except for participation in rebellion, or other crime, the basis of representation [in regards to the number

of state representatives to Congress] therein shall be reduced in the proportion which the number of such male citizens shall bear to the whole number of male citizens twenty-one years of age in such State.

The next section addressed the issue of Confederate generals and politicians who sought a government position in the United States government. The clause doesn't refer to the Confederate states in particular; rather, it states that no one who had "previously taken an oath" (as in a loyalty oath to serve the country) and then "engaged in insurrection or rebellion...or given aid or comfort to the enemies thereof" could hold office. This was a very punitive clause as far as the South was concerned. However, the amendment made a concession, saying that if two-thirds of Congress approved of someone, they would be allowed to take office.

In the fourth section, the public debt acquired throughout the war was validated. However, the United States did not hold itself responsible for the debt. "Neither the United States nor any State shall assume or pay any debt or obligation incurred in aid of insurrection or rebellion...or any claim for the loss or emancipation of any slave." The important phrase in this section is "or any claim for the loss or emancipation of any slave." In other words, no slave owner in the South would be compensated in any way for income or personal loss due to the freeing of the slaves. Remember, Lincoln and Johnson most likely would have approached this differently. Radical Republicans wanted nothing to do with compensating slave owners for what they considered to be an immoral act. In addition, the Fourteenth Amendment stated that the war debt was void. No state governments or even the federal government would reimburse the Confederate states for any war losses.

Finally, the amendment ends with "The Congress shall have the power to enforce, by appropriate legislation, the provisions of this article." Maybe you want to read that again. The Fourteenth

Amendment, which was designed to complete the Radical Reconstruction, had a way to reach through the centuries of American law and jurisprudence.

On June 16th, 1866, the Fourteenth Amendment was sent to the states for ratification. It took over two years for enough states to ratify it, and it was finally adopted on July 9th, 1868. Its purpose was to ensure equal civil rights for the emancipated slaves when it was adopted. Unfortunately, the South found ways around this for decades by using the notorious Black Codes, Jim Crow laws, and the future Supreme Court ruling of *Plessy v. Ferguson.*

The Fourteenth Amendment was the second of the three amendments that helped to abolish slavery and/or grant basic civil rights to the freed slaves and all blacks throughout the Union. The Fourteenth Amendment rejected the 1857 Dred Scott decision of the United States Supreme Court. That decision said that black men, born free or otherwise emancipated, did not share the same rights as whites according to the US Constitution. What this decision had denied to blacks, the Fourteenth Amendment granted to them.

After more than a century of the balance of power favoring the states, this amendment shifted that balance toward the federal government. This amendment is also the foundation of the Civil Rights Act of 1964 and the Voting Rights Act of 1965. Yet, if this amendment had been implemented to its fullest to begin with, those laws might never have been needed.

Before this amendment, the Supreme Court tended to rule in favor of the states on the questions of civil rights. After this amendment, the Supreme Court tended to rule in favor of maintaining the individual's civil rights. But this did not happen overnight. For instance, the *Plessy v. Ferguson* decision in 1896 was used for decades to validate the Jim Crow laws in the South.

Court Decisions Influenced by the Fourteenth Amendment

The Due Process Clause stated that not only did the federal government owe a citizen the due process of the law but so did the states. This Due Process Clause has been ruled on many times by the Supreme Court, expanding US citizens' rights almost every time. The Supreme Court has used this clause to protect individuals from infringement by states or the federal government.

The Equal Protection Clause and the Due Process Clause have been cited by the Supreme Court to expand protections for everything from the Bill of Rights to the right to privacy to the right to marry. The Equal Protection Clause was intended to keep the states from either legislating or approving of discrimination against blacks, and both of these clauses became the bulwarks for many landmark decisions.

Let's take a quick look at some of the Supreme Court's most important decisions that were influenced by these two clauses of the Fourteenth Amendment.

1925 – In *Gitlow v. New York*, the Supreme Court ruled that the Fourteenth Amendment extended the rights of the First Amendment, such as freedom of speech and freedom of the press, to state governments.

1954 – *Brown v. Board of Education* was a landmark case regarding civil rights. This case overturned the ruling of *Plessy v. Ferguson*, which stated "separate but equal." By using the Fourteenth Amendment, the Supreme Court declared that segregation in public schools did not meet the Equal Protection Clause's standards.

1965 – *Griswold v. Connecticut* paved the way for women to use contraception legally. This might seem like an odd case in regards to the Fourteenth Amendment, but a Supreme Court justice argued for the ruling by referring to the Due Process Clause, which protects the right to privacy.

1967 – *Loving v. Virginia* was another landmark case. The Supreme Court ruled that laws banning interracial marriage violated the Fourteenth Amendment and was unconstitutional.

1973 – This was the year the Supreme Court ruled on one of the most controversial cases it ever faced. The case was *Roe v. Wade*, and by using the Due Process Clause in the Fourteenth Amendment, the court found that laws against abortion violated a women's right to privacy. However, it left the book open on this by saying this right is not absolute and that it has to be balanced with the government's interests in protecting women's health and prenatal life.

2010 - *Obergefell v. Hodges* was another landmark decision. The Supreme Court ruled that the clauses in the Fourteenth Amendment upheld the right for same-sex couples to marry on the same terms as opposite-sex couples.

The Supreme Court has ruled that there are three protections provided by the Due Process Clause. They are:

1. Substantive Due Process – This allows courts to protect certain fundamental rights, even if they are not mentioned in the US Constitution.

2. Procedural Due Process – At its most basic definition, procedural due process means providing the person with notice, an opportunity to be heard, and a neutral person's decision. Many in the US are familiar with the Miranda warning; this is used to ensure procedural due process is being followed accordingly.

3. Vehicle for incorporating the Bill of Rights – Initially, the Supreme Court said that the Bill of Rights only applied to the federal government. However, they later ruled that the provisions in the Bill of Rights did apply to the states through the doctrine of incorporation in the Due Process Clause of the Fourteenth Amendment.

There has also been much debate regarding the citizenship clause over the years. Were children of immigrants automatically citizens? Was anyone born in the United States with parents that held citizenship elsewhere automatically a citizen? What about children born in the United States to diplomats from other countries? In the first two instances, the Supreme Court ruled that these children were citizens. However, a child born to foreign diplomats is not an automatic citizen. The Foreign Affairs Manual from the State Department makes it clear that "U.S. military installations abroad and U.S. diplomatic or consular facilities abroad are not part of the United States within the meaning of the Fourteenth Amendment."

By passing and ratifying the Fourteenth Amendment in 1868, the Radical Republican Congress believed they were addressing the Reconstruction's current needs. They had no idea of the amendment's importance when it came to shaping the future of the country and the validity of civil rights. Without this amendment, there may not have been a Civil Rights Act and a Voting Rights Act in the 1960s. Without this amendment, there would not have been the reading of the Miranda rights. Without this amendment, there might have been no right to privacy and no right to marry whoever you choose. It is unlikely the Radical Republicans had any inkling about the road they were setting the country on; however, due to the precedent they set, civil rights continued to move forward. Sadly, during their own time, civil rights stagnated, and although important bills were passed, they were never utilized to their fullest limits.

Chapter 10 – The Impeachment of Andrew Johnson, 1868

Many people are aware that Andrew Johnson was impeached by the House of Representatives and acquitted by the Senate. However, most of us do not understand why or what happened to instigate this action.

After Johnson declared Reconstruction to be over, Congress, which was run by the Radical Republicans, challenged him at every step. First, they created the Joint Committee on Reconstruction. Then they passed the Civil Rights Act of 1866 and the second Freedmen's Bureau bill, both of which the president vetoed. He also vetoed numerous Reconstruction Acts. However, Congress overruled him at almost every turn. As you can tell, there was much antagonism between the president and the sitting congressmen.

The passages of these bills and amendments angered white Southerners, which led to riots throughout the South. Many innocent former slaves were killed. Angry Northerners blamed President Johnson for this, believing he was too soft on the South.

Johnson proceeded to travel throughout the country, blaming the Radical Republicans, the blacks, and the pro-war Democrats for the ills of the reunited Union. This press tour is often referred to as

Johnson's "Swing Around the Circle." This effort failed, however, as it turned more Northerners to the Republicans in the 1866 elections. The Northerners were angry with Johnson for his pardons to Southern leaders and the fact that it seemed like blacks in the South were still "slaves," as the freed slaves were often working on the same plantations where they had once labored in the fields without any pay.

But what does all this have to do with the impeachment of Johnson? The actions of the House of Representatives were firmly rooted in the intense animosity between President Johnson and the Republican Congress. Congress continued to pass laws giving rights to freed slaves and restricting the activity of the South, while Johnson continued to veto them. Though the Republicans often had the votes to override Johnson's vetoes, they grew more irritated with his presidency every day. They looked for ways to fight back and eventually passed the Tenure of Office Act in 1867, which limited some presidential powers.

The Tenure of Office Act was actually passed in regards to Edward Stanton, the Secretary of War, who was a Radical Republican. Stanton had been Lincoln's choice for the position of secretary of war, so Johnson inherited him. Johnson inherited many Republicans, but none stood in his way as much as Stanton did. Congress was worried Stanton would be replaced, so they passed this act in 1867 to ensure he wouldn't be dismissed without reason. This act called for the president to seek the Senate's consent before dismissing any members of his Cabinet.

Johnson tried to force Stanton's resignation but failed to do so. In the summer of 1867, while Congress was in recess, President Johnson suspended Stanton, and Ulysses S. Grant was chosen to take his place. This move was allowed under the Tenure of Office Act, but it was something that Congress was not expecting. When the Senate met back up later that year, they said they did not concur with the decision. Grant said he would resign, as he feared a legal battle would ensue, but Johnson convinced him to stay. When the Senate voted to reinstate Stanton in January of the next year, Grant immediately stepped to the side, leading to a breakdown between him and Johnson. However, it was due to these actions that Grant became the frontrunner for the 1868 presidential election, which he would go on to win.

Johnson searched for someone else to fill the spot, but instead of compromising, he simply chose someone who he knew would be loyal to him. The interim secretary of war, Lorenzo Thomas, hand-delivered Stanton's dismissal letter to him, but Stanton refused to leave his post, citing the Tenure of Office Act.

The Senate was outraged. The president had challenged a congressional order, and the House of Representatives quickly wrote up articles of impeachment, charging Johnson with "high crimes and misdemeanors."

The House voted to impeach 126 to 47, but the majority of the Senate voted for acquittal. Johnson survived by one single vote. At that time, Johnson did not have a vice president. If he had been removed from office, the Senate's pro tempore would have been next in line for the presidency, unlike today when the Speaker of the House would ascend to the presidency.

Andrew Johnson was the first of only three US presidents to be impeached (so far, no US president has been convicted on these terms). The political implications of this action shifted the balance of power again between the executive and legislative branches. Congress could not impeach a president just because they didn't like his policies. But, at the same time, the impeachment diminished the president's power.

There were other fallouts from the impeachment trial. No Republican senator who voted to acquit ever served in public office again, and Johnson's presidency was essentially over. The Tenure of Office Act was repealed in 1887, and the Supreme Court deemed the act to be unconstitutional in 1926 during the case of *Myers v. United States.*

Chapter 11 – The Fifteenth Amendment, 1870

Ulysses S. Grant was elected president in 1868, although he wouldn't take office until the following March. There was a lot of concern in the Republican Party regarding their possible success in future elections. Most Republicans believed that the Democrats would see a resurgence, and they knew they needed the black vote to stay in power.

So, on February 26th, 1869, Congress passed a compromised version of the Fifteenth Amendment. The final version banned any restrictions on voting based on race, color, or previous servitude.

However, the amendment was a far cry from the original wording. Representative John Bingham, who helped draft the Fourteenth Amendment, pushed for an amendment that included bans on the basis of "race, color, nativity, property, education, or religious beliefs." There was also a clause to ban literacy tests. Prejudice was strong everywhere, not just in the South. The North had an influx of foreign-born citizens, and some House representatives (both in the North and in the West) did not want them to be able to easily vote. In addition, both Southern and Northern Republicans wanted those Southerners who had supported the Confederacy to still be banned from voting; they believed this amendment would make it easier for them to gain their right to vote.

Because of all the infighting, the House and the Senate passed different versions of the amendment, which meant that a House and Senate conference committee had to meet to hammer out the differences and produce the amendment's final wording. In the interest of getting the amendment ratified by the necessary number of states, the more controversial language, such as guaranteeing blacks could hold office or banning poll taxes, were not included.

The House approved of the new wording on February 25th, 1869, with the Senate approving the measure the next day. The House saw 35 representatives abstain from voting, while 144 members voted for it. Forty-four members voted against it. The vote in the Senate was 39 to 13, with 14 senators abstaining. Thirteen Radical Republican senators refused to vote because the amendment was not what they had envisioned, and they wanted something that would benefit blacks more. Despite this, the amendment passed.

The wording of the amendment is short and simple, but its impact has been felt down through the years. Much blood, tears, and heartbreak has been shed and felt because of it. The amendment simply states:

> Section 1. The right of citizens of the United States to vote shall not be denied or abridged by the United States or by any State on account of race, color, or previous condition of servitude.

> Section 2. The Congress shall have power to enforce this article by appropriate legislation.

Opposition to this amendment also came from the women's suffrage movement. Before and during the Civil War, the women's suffrage movement had been aligned with the abolitionist movement. The Fourteenth Amendment left women feeling that their rights were not important, as only male rights were protected. Some women wanted to continue their work and make sure African Americans got the equality they deserved, while other prominent women, such as Susan B. Anthony and Elizabeth Cady Stanton, wanted rights extended to women at the same time.

Things got worse with the proposal of the Fifteenth Amendment because it barred race discrimination but not sex discrimination. This caused a rift in the movement, as the women now knew they had to choose which issue to prioritize first. This split the American Equal Rights Association in two. The new organizations became rivals, with the National Woman Suffrage Association, led by Susan B. Anthony and Elizabeth Cady Stanton, rejecting the Fifteenth Amendment. The American Woman Suffrage Association, led by Lucy Stone and an African American woman named Frances Ellen Watkins Harper, supported the amendment.

But the amendment wouldn't be a reality until enough states ratified it. On March 1ˢᵗ, 1869, Nevada became the first state to ratify the Fifteenth Amendment. Within a few months, most of the Midwestern and New England states had ratified it as well. Some of the Southern states in which the Radical Republicans still had control also ratified it quickly.

To get the last few needed states, Congress passed several Reconstruction acts that made it mandatory for the states of Virginia, Mississippi, Texas, and Georgia to ratify the amendment before sending representatives to Congress again. By February 1870, all four states had ratified the amendment. On February 3ʳᵈ, 1870, twenty-eight states had ratified the amendment, and it became a part of the Constitution. Iowa was the last of the twenty-eight states to do so, following the example of Georgia, which had passed it just the day before.

Abolitionist organizations and black communities celebrated, as many considered this event to be the end of Reconstruction and a moment where black rights were secured for future generations.

The Republicans were so confident that they even proclaimed black men no longer needed the federal government's protection. Many abolitionist organizations disbanded, and James A. Garfield, who would later become the president, said the amendment's passage "confers upon the African race the care of its destiny. It places their fortunes in their own hands." Unfortunately, they were wrong. It was certainly a major accomplishment for black civil rights, but it was not the end of their story, nor was it the end of Reconstruction.

It was still a great moment in history when, on March 31st, 1870, Thomas Mundy Peterson cast his vote in New Jersey, becoming the first black man to vote due to the provisions of the Fifteenth Amendment. This was followed by the election of many blacks to public office, as black men took advantage of their newly protected rights. Around 2,000 black men held local, state, and federal offices throughout the country, with sixteen serving in Congress.

While the Fifteenth Amendment granted black men the right to vote, states, particularly in the South, made it difficult for them to cast their ballot. This can be seen in the following court cases, which required the US Supreme Court to weigh in.

Judicial Reviews

1876 – *United States v. Reese* was probably the most important case in regards to the limitations that would be placed on blacks in the years to come. In 1873, two election inspectors refused to allow an African American man to vote in an election in Kentucky. They stated that the man had refused to pay the poll tax, even though the man had tried to pay it but was refused. They also refused his affidavit, which would have excused the non-paid poll tax under the Enforcement Act of 1870 (this act prohibited officials from discriminating against those trying to vote based on race or color). The two election inspectors were charged with violating the Enforcement Act, but instead of reinforcing that act, the Supreme Court decided the wording in the Enforcement Act was too broad and didn't fit in the context of the Fifteenth Amendment. The justices interpreted the amendment much more narrowly. They ruled that the Fifteenth Amendment didn't actually "grant the right of suffrage"; rather, it prohibited the states "from giving preference...to one citizen of the United States over another on account of race, color, or previous condition of servitude...If citizens of one race having certain qualifications are permitted by law to vote, those of another having the same qualifications must be."

This ruling led to states, particularly in the South, to pass laws that excluded blacks, as well as poor white men, from voting. Literacy tests and poll taxes became commonplace over time. Grandfather clauses were also in place in some states, which exempted voters from these voting requirements if their grandfathers had been able to vote. These measures were not limited to the South. This Supreme Court ruling also led the Ku Klux Klan and other white supremacists to use violence and intimidation to keep blacks from voting, which will be covered in more depth in the next chapter.

As the Supreme Court continued to interpret the Fifteenth Amendment more narrowly, Southern states adopted new constitutions and new laws to set conditions for voting registration. It was not until the early 1900s that the Supreme Court began to give a broader interpretation to the Fifteenth Amendment.

1915 – In *Guinn v. the United States,* the Supreme Court struck down the grandfather clause that had allowed whites, especially those who were poorer and illiterate, to bypass poll taxes and literacy tests.

1927 – The Supreme Court struck down a Texas law that forbade blacks from voting in the Texas Democratic primary in *Nixon v. Herndon.* Dr. Lawrence Nixon, who was African American, would later bring another case to the Supreme Court in 1932, which again challenged the idea of an all-white Democratic primary in Texas. It was only in 1944, in *Smith v. Allwright,* that white primaries in Texas were deemed unconstitutional, which, in turn, affected other states.

1960 – *Gomillion v. Lightfoot* ruled that a gerrymandered district, which aimed to exclude black voters, violated the Fifteenth Amendment. Gerrymandering is not a thing of the past, as it still happens today, but redrawing lines to disenfranchise racial and ethnic minorities is not allowed. While Gerrymandering based on party lines is allowed, many argue that this is a fine line, as they can still affect racial and ethnic minorities.

This amendment continued to play a major role in validating the civil rights acts in the 1960s. For instance, in 1965, Congress passed the Voting Rights Act. This act addressed many of the ways that Southern states had disenfranchised black voters, despite the rights laid out in previous amendments. The Voting Rights Act outlawed literacy tests and established the federal government's oversight of voter registration in the areas where the majority of black residents were not registered. It also allowed the US attorney general to investigate other disenfranchisement tools, such as the poll tax.

Chapter 12 – The Ku Klux Klan Act, 1871

Most people have seen the pictures and heard the stories. Out of the darkness of the night would come hooded horseman or people on foot, who would then burn crosses in front of houses, beat up unsuspecting blacks, and terrorize the black community by hanging black men from trees. These masked men were known as the Ku Klux Klan or, more simply as, the KKK.

In late December 1865, former Confederate officers of the Civil War founded a secret social fraternity named the Ku Klux Klan. The Klan did not stay a social fraternity for long, as it soon warped into a violent terror group with a paramilitary attitude. The Klan's goal was to reverse everything the federal government had achieved during Reconstruction. Their main focus was to repress the rights of former slaves and all black people.

But why the name Ku Klux Klan? It is thought they used the Greek word *kyklos*, meaning circle, in combination with the word "clan." For a short time, the Klan was known as the Kuklux Clan. The first grand wizard of the KKK was a former confederate general named Nathan Bedford Forrest. Forrest eventually tired of the Klan's violence and tried to disband it, although he was unsuccessful. Late in life, he claimed he had never even been a part of the organization, although this claim is false.

Black Americans were not the only ones targeted by the Klan. Anyone who assisted them or stood up for them was also vulnerable. This was particularly true of white Republicans living in the South. The Klan destroyed property and assaulted and murdered their victims to intimidate blacks from voting in elections.

When the Union soldiers were still in the South, they could break up the Klan activities. In 1870, Congress passed the First Ku Klux Act (also known as the Enforcement Act). This act prohibited discrimination in regards to voting. This act even gave the president the right to deploy the military if rebellions broke out due to this act. The Second Enforcement Act was passed in 1871, and it continued to help protect the voting rights of African Americans.

The last Enforcement Act (known as the Third Enforcement Act, the Third Ku Klux Klan Act, or simply the Ku Klux Klan Act) was also passed in 1871. This piece of legislation gave the president the authority to suspend the writ of *habeas corpus* (under which people could report unlawful imprisonment to a court) in order to fight the Klan and other white supremacist groups. It was brought to the House by Republican Representative Samuel Shellabarger from Ohio, and it passed the House on April 6th. It was amended and then sent to the Senate, where it passed, becoming law on April 20th, 1871.

Opponents of the bill considered it unconstitutional, as they believed it violated the rights of state governments to control their elections. Others expressed the opposite sentiments, as the violence of the Klan and other white supremacist groups were incredibly harmful to the American public, particularly the black populace. Six months after signing the bill into law, Grant used its provisions in South Carolina. Martial law was declared in nine South Carolina counties, and the military arrested hundreds of alleged Klansmen.

Due to this move, the Klan disappeared in South Carolina and elsewhere in the South.

If you try to find this act in its entirety today, you won't find it. The act has undergone many revisions, with portions of the act expiring after the Reconstruction. The Supreme Court's narrow interpretation also impacted the effects of the law, as most of their rulings stated that the law only applied to the states. In 1883, the Supreme Court found some of this legislation to be unconstitutional.

By that time, though, the Klan had faded into the background, although it would come back years later in 1915, this time with a focus on persecuting not just blacks but also Catholics, Jews, and immigrants. This revival would slowly fade away in the 1940s before rising yet again in full force in the 1950s and 1960s to fight the civil rights movement. Some chapters of the Ku Klux Klan have survived to this day, and there is a movement to label the group as a terrorist organization.

Chapter 13 – The Civil Rights Act of 1875

Three years after the passage of the Ku Klux Klan Act, Congress felt the need for another act to help protect African American civil rights and passed the Civil Rights Act of 1875. Once again, Congress was attempting to enforce the rights of all citizens, particularly those that were outlined in the Thirteenth, Fourteenth, and Fifteenth Amendments.

This act was drafted by Radical Republican Senator Charles Sumner and John Mercer Langston, an African American who would become the first president of Virginia State University and the first dean at Howard University. The last name of Langston might sound familiar to some; his brother was the grandfather of the well-known poet Langston Hughes. Although the bill was drafted in 1870, it did not get passed until 1875. By this time, Sumner had died, and many saw the act as a way to memorialize his work. Although Grant signed the law, he didn't agree with it. He and Sumner had never seen eye to eye, and Grant did nothing to ensure the law was enforced effectively. The federal government did not send copies to United States attorneys around the country, and federal courts ruled that it was unconstitutional long before the US

Supreme Court issued their ruling. Public opinion on the bill was split right down the color line, with whites opposing it and blacks supporting it. It was overwhelmingly opposed in newspaper editorials around the country.

The law was intended to provide equal treatment to all citizens in regards to public transportation and to stop blacks from being excluded from jury service. It also included a clause that stated any lawsuits coming from civil rights violations must be heard in federal courts, not state or local courts. However, Grant had wanted a law that would help suppress the violence related to black voting rights in the South. The Reconstruction was on its last legs by this point, and it would end about two years later. The Civil Rights Act of 1875 would be the last major piece of legislation related to Reconstruction.

The law read, in part, "all persons within the jurisdiction of the United States shall be entitled to the full and equal enjoyment of the accommodations, advantages, facilities, and privileges of inns, public conveyances on land or water, theaters, and other places of public amusement; subject only to the conditions and limitations established by law, and applicable alike to citizens of every race and color."

As you can see, the public accommodation clause was at the heart of the act. Unfortunately, the Supreme Court ruled this section of the act unconstitutional in 1883 in the *Civil Rights Cases*, which was a group of five cases related to civil rights. The Supreme Court said the Equal Protection Clause of the Fourteenth Amendment, which this bill enforced, did not prohibit discrimination by individuals or organizations. It only prohibits local or state governments from discriminating. They also ruled that the Thirteenth Amendment was meant to ensure blacks were no longer seen as slaves; according to the majority of the justices, it did not have anything to do with discrimination in public accommodations. Thus, segregation would remain in place until the 1960s. In 1964 and 1968, two new acts were passed, and parts of the Civil Rights Act of 1875 were incorporated into them.

Long-Term Impact

As noted above, this was the last major piece of civil rights legislation during the Reconstruction era. In fact, it would be the last federal civil rights act until 1957.

It appears that the public in the North and the South had grown tired of the Reconstruction. They wanted it over with, even if that meant embracing segregation. However, blacks saw this act as an important piece of legislation. In 1874, while the bill was being debated in the House of Representatives, African American Representative James Rapier from Alabama stood up and said, "I have no compromise to offer on this subject...After all, this question resolves itself into this: either I am a man or I am not a man."

Even though this act had little impact when it was enacted, it would find new life almost ninety years later in the 1960s with the passage of some of the most influential civil rights acts.

Chapter 14 – The Compromise of 1877

The politics of 1877 were drastically different from when the Radical Republicans took over Congress and impeached Andrew Johnson back in the late 1860s. This was perfectly exemplified by the elections of 1877. By this year, people in both the North and the South were tired and wanted the Reconstruction to be over, and there was little support for any more legislation for advantageous racially inspired policies.

Southern whites were more than fed up with the Reconstruction and still used violence and intimidation to prevent blacks from voting, serving on juries, or using public accommodations. Northerners had other things on their plates that they thought needed to be prioritized. The Gilded Age was beginning to bloom, and with that came new business ventures and labor strikes; issues of the economy were coming to the forefront, while civil rights were getting pushed back. Many white Northerners thought they had done enough to secure liberties for blacks. They thought the issue now lay with Southern governments. Others thought it could not be achieved, as their efforts often led to violence and the dissolution of their policies. The Supreme Court struck down many provisions of the Thirteenth and Fourteenth Amendments and narrowly interpreted other acts; it seemed this would be a never-ending battle. There were also many accusations of corruption within the Grant administration, which made an already weary public turn against the Republican Party, which had been in power since Lincoln was inaugurated in 1861.

Of course, the problem with leaving the cause of civil rights in the hands of the South was that many white Southerners did not care about the advancement of African Americans, which was reflected in government politics. Regardless, by 1877, there was just no appetite left in the North for fighting these inequities.

Before the Compromise of 1877

Throughout the 19th century, America was a country of compromises in an attempt to blend the very different worlds of slavery and non-slavery and of the agricultural South and the industrial North. Parts of the country threatened to secede numerous times during the century, and every time except for one, the government was able to make compromises that prevented the nation from splitting apart.

The compromises can be seen in the US government's earliest history. Right from the start—within the Constitution itself—these compromises were front and center. This compromise was reached in 1787 during the Constitutional Convention. The convention's delegates had argued bitterly over the issue of slavery and the question of congressional representation. The North did not want the South to be able to count their slaves toward the population, which would be used to determine congressional representation. Of course, the South demanded to count all persons, including the slaves. The North believed that this would give the South an unfair allocation due to the many enslaved people in the South.

This was a major roadblock to passing the Constitution, and a compromise had to be reached. Eventually, the delegates came up with the Three-Fifths Compromise, in which the slaves in the South were to be counted as three-fifths of a person for the purposes of congressional representation. Another way of looking at it was to count three out of every five slaves. And yet another way of looking at it is that the American public, for the most part, actually saw slaves as three-fifths of a person. This completely dehumanized the slave population, and it took over one hundred years for America to realize what had been "best" for the American public in 1787 was no longer the case. Of course, it was not best for the slaves or the black population in general, and sadly, this mentality was passed down through the generations.

Another significant compromise regarding slavery was the Missouri Compromise of 1820. The Missouri Compromise was another attempt to keep the Union together. As Missouri moved to become a state, many involved simply assumed it would be a pro-slavery state. However, many abolitionists and Republicans vigorously fought against another slave state from entering the Union. After much wrangling, Congress passed the Missouri Compromise. The compromise allowed Missouri to enter the Union as a slave state but banned all slavery north of the 36° 30' parallel. This compromise was enacted after President James Monroe signed it in 1820.

The next major compromise was the Compromise of 1850. The Compromise of 1850 actually refers to five different bills. These dealt with the land the United States had acquired with its victory in the Mexican-American War. This territory included the modern-day states of New Mexico, Arizona, Utah, Nevada, California, and a part of Colorado. Once again, the question of slavery found its way to the top of this discussion. California would be admitted as a free state, while the other territories would have to figure out their stance on slavery. The Compromise of 1850 also reinforced the Fugitive Slave Act of 1793. Law enforcement was supposed to arrest anyone suspected of being a fugitive slave. Anyone who did not arrest an alleged fugitive slave would be subjected to a fine, as would those aiding runaway slaves.

The final compromise before the Civil War broke out was the Nebraska-Kansas Act. In 1854, the Nebraska-Kansas Act was passed to open up these lands for the transcontinental railroad. However, it is most remembered for repealing the Missouri Compromise of 1820.

Since it no longer mattered if a state was above or below the 36° 30' parallel, both anti-slavery and pro-slavery advocates moved to Kansas in an effort to be the deciding populace regarding slavery in the new state. These battles between pro-slavery and anti-slavery groups grew more violent, eventually resulting in Bleeding Kansas. Kansas would be admitted as a free state in 1861, but many in the nation knew that the issue of slavery would lead to war, just as it had in Kansas.

The Compromise of 1877

The Compromise of 1877 was different than the others that came before it in two ways.

1. It was put in place after the Civil War. All the other compromises had been reached before the war in an attempt to prevent the Southern states from seceding. It is interesting to note that this compromise had the same goal as the first three—to hold the Union together.

2. The Compromise of 1877 was not worked out in the halls of Congress with vigorous debates and passionate speeches. No, this compromise was worked on behind closed doors. It was the result of a disputed and chaotic presidential election, during which both the North and the South accused each other of fraud. Old issues had reared their ugly heads to taint the election's results.

The presidential election of 1876 was filled with much tension. Many thought Grant would run for a third time, and when he decided not to do so, there was a mad dash to find a strong candidate. That candidate was Rutherford B. Hayes, and he went up against Democratic candidate Samuel Tilden. The number of electoral votes needed at that time was 185. Tilden ended up with 184 electoral votes, while Hayes had 165. The problem was that the remaining four states who had to report their counts were struck by voter fraud. For instance, in South Carolina, 101 percent of voters cast a vote. Tilden had a huge lead in the popular vote, but the Republicans refused to concede. They claimed fraud had occurred in the South, as both African Americans and Republicans were intimidated into not voting. The voting in South Carolina was marred with violence on both sides. Clashes between whites and blacks resulted in the deaths of five people. In a town near Charleston, violence took the lives of six white men when black men opened fire inside a political meeting.

While three of the contested states were in the South, the other one was in the West. Oregon's electoral vote seemed to be in Hayes's favor, but the governor claimed that one of the electors was ineligible, replacing the former Republican elector with a Democratic one. All of this threw the election into chaos. As a result, Rutherford B. Hayes became the first and so far the only president ever to be decided by an Electoral Commission.

Before getting into the specifics of the Compromise of 1877, it is interesting to look at who scholars think won the election. It is certainly hard to know for certain, as the election was not conducted fairly in the South, but more than likely, Hayes would have won Oregon, South Carolina, and Louisiana, while Tilden would have won Florida. If this had been the case, scholars think Hayes would have won not only the electoral vote but also the popular vote.

Here is what happened when the Democrats and Republicans met in private at the Wormley Hotel in Washington, DC. In order to give the election to Hayes, it is believed the Democrats demanded:

- The removal of all federal troops from Louisiana, South Carolina, and Florida. This move would effectively end the Reconstruction, as all Southern states would then be under home rule.

- The appointment of a Southern Democrat to the Cabinet. Hayes appointed an ex-Confederate as the postmaster general. This move was not popular in the North or with the Northern Republicans, who still controlled the Senate.

- The provision of federal funds and assistance to industrialize the South in an attempt to boost the Southern economy. Southern ports were still devastated, and even Mississippi River shipping was down to nothing.

- The federal government would provide funding for a transcontinental railway across the South.

- The federal government would not interfere with racial issues in the South. This might have been the point that had the most ramifications over the decades.

It is not known for certain what deals were made at the Wormley Hotel, but scholars are fairly certain these were the key points. Regardless, the inauguration of Rutherford Hayes, which took place peacefully on March 5th, 1877, effectively ended the Reconstruction.

Although Hayes said he was committed to a Southern route for the railroad, he did not keep this promise. However, Southern Democrats did not live up to their commitment to "recognize the civil and political equality of blacks." The Democrats in the South proceeded to pass various taxes and laws that greatly affected African Americans. Blacks felt that the Republican Party had betrayed them, as the South fell under Democratic rule until the 1960s.

Was the Compromise of 1877 worth the price each side paid? Was the presidency worth giving up the fight for equal rights? Most Republicans thought so. It seems their thinking was short-sighted. A president typically served eight years (two terms) back then, but safeguarding civil rights, especially according to our modern viewpoint, would have been the heroic and right thing to do. After this election, the Democrats would own the "Solid South" until the 1980s, which was when the Republicans again took over. It should be noted that over time, the two parties also slowly switched values. Most scholars believe this started to happen in 1936 when Franklin Delano Roosevelt, a Democrat, was re-elected for the second time. The Democratic Party, which used to advocate for a strong state government, began advocating for a strong central government, in addition to increased civil rights.

However, the compromise of 1877 did keep the Union in one piece, but nothing would be the same. Democrats learned quickly that the old South before the war was not coming back, and it also did not bring the South onto equal terms with the North regarding the economy, social order, and political standing. However, it did dictate that white rule and influence would prevail in the South for generations to come. This rule was held together by the oppression, intimidation, and segregation of the millions of African Americans who lived in those states.

In 1877, the military forces of the North left the South, which resulted in widespread disenfranchisement of blacks and the new Jim Crow laws. Segregation ruled in the South until Lyndon Baines Johnson's administration took over following President John F. Kennedy's assassination.

Chapter 15 – The Official End of the Reconstruction

The end of Reconstruction wasn't pretty. It wasn't well organized. And it wasn't planned. You could say the country had simply grown weary of the Reconstruction efforts and wanted it to be over. The anger and bitterness caused by the Civil War had essentially subsided, and Republicans began to back away from their commitments to racial equality in the South and the broad powers of the federal government that was needed to accomplish it.

Over time, the Republicans had become less "radical" and more conservative. For many Republicans, the Radical Reconstruction looked like a misguided adventure. To them, it seemed like a time filled with failed attempts to raise the standard of living for blacks and the poor in the South. Thus, the Republicans in 1876 and 1877 began to see the Reconstruction as a fading era and chose to abandon it.

As the Republicans backed away, white Democratic local and state governments began to take over. Many complained that the Reconstruction had banned the leaders of the Confederacy—both civilian and military—from political life. Many blamed this ban for the state of affairs in the South as Reconstruction moved toward its end. With many Republicans moving back north, the South was unstable and full of corruption in its state governments.

In addition to these factors, the Panic of 1873 triggered an economic depression, and Northerners no longer found it profitable to be guardians for the ex-slaves. It seemed that the economy had to take center stage for everyone to get the nation back on an even financial keel.

As the economy declined, the Stalwart Republicans replaced the Radical Republicans. The country was bone-weary from the political and physical violence of the Reconstruction. These Republicans were not interested in controlling or punishing the South anymore. They were concerned with the economy, corruption in public life, and trade. Over the years, the Radical Republicans had become leaderless, and they drifted apart as different factions arose. This had opened the door for the Stalwart Republicans, of which many former Radical Republicans joined the ranks, as they wanted to take a more cautious approach to politics.

The Democrats also changed. Dubbing themselves the Redeemers, the New Departure Democrats moved away from the pro-slavery Democrats and the former Copperheads. The Copperheads had been Democrats who opposed the Civil War and wanted a peace settlement made with the Confederates. They dissolved in 1868, shortly after the war ended. The New Departure Democrats were also focused on the economy, business, trade, and corruption, particularly in the Southern governments. Their goals meshed well with the changes in the Republican Party. These Democrats gained home rule in the South and declared that the best government was a local government. For Southerners, this meant an all-white government, with no room for ex-slaves or even white Republicans. With these policies in place, Reconstruction ended in some Southern states, such as Virginia, Tennessee, and Georgia.

The Depression of 1873 lasted for six years and destroyed the last vestiges of Northern interest in the Reconstruction. In both the North and the South, the depression hit hard. Labor unions died out, and Southerners lost their farms and land. Wages fell, and debt and bankruptcies grew all over the country. The Democrats used this environment to take control of the House of Representatives in 1874, doing so for the first time since the Civil War began.

It was easier for the Democrats to gain control during this time because of all the corruption going on in Grant's administration. The most well-known incident was the Whiskey Ring in 1875, in which government officials stole millions of dollars in a tax evasion scam. But there were problems before this. In 1869, Grant was tied to the Black Friday scandal, in which speculators became close to Grant and learned inside secrets, manipulating the market and ruining the economy. This scandal was not the sole reason for the Panic of 1873, but it did contribute to it. These scandals led the public to distrust Grant and, in turn, the Republicans.

Because of these changes in the political environment, the Reconstruction officially ended when President Rutherford B. Hayes withdrew all Union troops from the Southern states of North Carolina, Florida, and Louisiana after assuming office. From here on, the promises of the Radical Reconstruction fell by the wayside, and the Reconstruction officially died. Unfortunately, the violence and discrimination in the South meant most blacks couldn't vote, and few held public office. In the decades that followed the end of Reconstruction, blacks faced even worse hardships and discrimination. It would take until the 1960s for any of that to truly change.

Chapter 16 – After the Reconstruction

The end of the Reconstruction era came abruptly after the Compromise of 1877. To many, though, the Reconstruction seemed to stagger to its death.

The period that followed the end of the Reconstruction was deemed "the Redemption" by white Southerners. This period was certainly not geared toward the black residents of the South. Democratic local and state governments were finally free to organize life in the South the way they wanted it. And they wanted segregation and discrimination.

The Jim Crow Laws

The new Democratic state governments across the South passed a variety of Jim Crow laws. Much like the earlier Black Codes, the Jim Crow laws were meant to incarcerate and segregate blacks as much as possible and keep them from voting.

But who was Jim Crow? It is believed that there was never actually a person named this. The name came from a song and dance routine, which was created before the Civil War even broke out. It has been thought that the name Jim Crow came from a man named Jim Cuff (although it's possible his name was actually Jim Crow), who was a disabled slave. The song was meant to be entertaining, but it mocked black people, especially as the song and dance was performed by a white man in black face. Around 1840, the term "Jim Crow" was used to refer to black people, and white politicians simply adopted the name after the Reconstruction era had ended.

The Jim Crow laws were responsible for the segregation of public facilities and institutions. These included schools, theaters, public bathrooms, and water fountains, just to name a few. This means there was two of everything, as there needed to be one for whites and one for blacks. Although it seemed as if the South was upholding the future ruling of *Plessy v. Ferguson* ("separate but equal"), that wasn't the case. The black facilities were far less in quality than the white facilities. African Americans were targeted by whites for minor infractions, and the laws often didn't look kindly in their favor, even if they were in the right. Blacks couldn't vote, serve on juries, or hold public office. In other words, things were certainly not "separate but equal." The next chapter will discuss the Supreme Court decision of *Plessy v. Ferguson* in more detail, but it was a monumental case that took place in 1896, about twenty years after Reconstruction had ended. This doctrine held sway for decades until the civil rights movement of the 1950s and 1960s. It should also be noted that these laws could be found elsewhere in the United States, but they were primarily focused, as well as harsher, in the South.

In Louisiana, in 1900, the black community was the largest population group in the state. Yet less than 5,500 were in the voter registration books. This continued to decrease until there were only 730 registered African Americans. In North Carolina, from 1896 to 1904, the black community was completely purged from the voter rolls. Black people were essentially invisible within the political system. Since you had to be a registered voter to run for office or serve on a jury, this meant blacks were excluded from doing these things. Not having African Americans in office meant blacks had no voice as far as politics were concerned. And not having blacks on juries often meant African Americans would be tried by all-white juries who could be quick to condemn based on just their skin color. It also helped to encourage whites to engage in violence against the black community, such as lynching, as they knew there would often be no repercussions for their actions.

For the most part, the courts upheld the legislation, new constitutions, and actions by the Southern states. During this time period, the complete suppression of the black vote ensured that the white Democrats would remain in control. It was a time of cruelty and oppression for black Southerners and even their white allies.

Despite all the talk in the years after Reconstruction about a new South, it remained very close to the old pre-war South. Southern blacks were free, but what did that freedom mean if you had no job, no money, no home, and no hope of changing things? Small groups of black men found work in the foundries and mills, forming iron and steel. They were banned from working in the rapidly growing textile mills. These textile mills were owned by whites, who chose to hire women and even children before hiring a black man.

The South was able to institutionalize segregation in housing, public accommodations, and public schools by 1900. When they were challenged, the Supreme Court upheld the Jim Crow laws. This legal segregation allowed whites to feel superior to "inferior blacks." The myths about black laziness, which had been around since the time of slavery but which was amplified during this time, and the institutionalization of segregation allowed for an atmosphere of violence. Lynchings became almost commonplace, along with whippings, things that would have been similar to what the slaves had endured.

Because the Southern white establishment feared the African Americans banding together and taking charge (which, if they had been able to do so, they would have been able to take the reins of power quite easily as they outnumbered the whites), they looked for ways to deny African Americans their voting rights. This was where poll taxes and literacy tests came into play. If you recall, these types of tactics were intentionally left out of the Fourteenth Amendment.

An excellent example of the situation blacks found themselves in was in Mississippi in 1890. The state constitution placed limits on voting rights, which included excluding anyone who had been convicted of a crime (including vagrancy), residency requirements, poll taxes and payment of all other taxes, and the infamous literacy test. These were all enshrined in the Mississippi Constitution.

There were, of course, loopholes designed so poor and uneducated whites could be able to vote. These were the grandfather clauses that allowed anyone whose ancestors had been registered to be registered as well. Another example of a loophole can be seen in those white people who couldn't read. They would be allowed to vote if they could show that they understood the Constitution. Eventually, the grandfather clauses were stripped away by the Supreme Court, but the states found other ways to prevent blacks from voting.

The Black Community after Reconstruction

Blacks certainly had a hard life, but the people responded in different ways. Many left the South for the North, while a few went to Africa. In some states, blacks were able to establish their own towns, which were composed entirely of African Americans. These were primarily in Kansas, Oklahoma, and Tennessee. Some organized or were a part of movements like the National Afro-American League (1890–1908).

There were great differences in the black community about the best way to reclaim their civil rights. Two men, W. E. B. Du Bois and Booker T. Washington, best personify these differences.

Washington was the founder of the Tuskegee Institute, in addition to being an author and advisor, while Du Bois was a philosopher, sociologist, and writer. Washington favored a course where blacks would become independent of whites by concentrating on improving themselves within the economy. He felt the time spent challenging discrimination or fighting for equality only took away from African American economic growth. In 1903, Du Bois wrote *The Souls of Black Folks,* in which he attacked Booker T. Washington's position. Du Bois believed that education was vital and more than a trade apprenticeship. He wanted blacks to have access to every level of formal education, including higher education. He advocated for intelligent, well-educated blacks to change the system by voting where it was allowed and protesting where it was not.

Education had been expanding in these years, with the Morrill Act of 1862 creating both white and black colleges. The next Morrill Act in 1890 provided more funding for these schools and also forbade racial discrimination. Of course, the black community truly did not benefit from expanding public education until many decades later. By 1900, it is believed that over 2,000 blacks had earned higher-education degrees.

The new immigration that followed the post-war industrial rise was a slap in the face to Southern blacks, who were still locked into a segregated society. Although these immigrants faced many hardships, they were more easily accepted into the melting pot of America while blacks struggled to survive. These immigrants faced prejudice, some of which endures to this day, and this influx also brought about a short revival of the Ku Klux Klan, as they opposed immigration. Native Americans also felt immigration was overall negative in regards to their place in American society.

In general, life was not much better for non-whites in the South after the Reconstruction, and it would not get better for many decades.

Chapter 17 – Plessy v. Ferguson: Separate but Equal, 1896

Although *Plessy v. Ferguson* took place after Reconstruction, it is an excellent example of how the black civil rights movement had stunted. This was a landmark case that the Supreme Court ruled on, and their ruling on the matter would be the guiding light for decades, allowing suffering and inequities to non-whites to occur.

The year was 1896, and the question before the Supreme Court was the constitutionality of racial segregation. This was the historic case that made "separate but equal" accommodations the law of the South until the 1960s, which was when this decision was overruled. With respect to where America is now regarding racism and equality, this Supreme Court ruling might be the most influential decision the court ever made, even though it was overturned.

The plaintiff, Homer Plessy, was a resident of New Orleans. He was mixed race (he was one-eighth black, seven-eighths white). Plessy was fair-skinned, but under Louisiana law, he was considered to be black, which meant he had to adhere to the strict laws put in place for segregation. One such law had been passed in 1890. This was the Separate Car Act, which required separate accommodations on trains for white and non-white riders. In 1892, Homer deliberately broke the law while boarding a train car labeled "whites only."

On June 7th, 1892, Plessy took part in an orchestrated move to test the limits of this law, which was coordinated by the Comité des Citoyens ("Citizens' Committee"). This was a diverse group fighting against racial discrimination in a world that constantly put whites first. First, Plessy bought a ticket for a first-class seat at the Press Street Depot in New Orleans. He then boarded the whites-only car that was going to Covington, Louisiana, on the East Louisiana Railroad. The railroad had been notified in advance that Plessy intended to challenge the law. The company itself actually opposed the law because it required them to add more cars.

The Comité des Citoyens hired a private detective so he could confront and detain Plessy when he boarded the train car. The group was worried that if someone else had apprehended Plessy, he might be charged with something like vagrancy instead of being charged for violating the Separate Car Act. After Plessy took his seat in the whites-only car, the detective ordered him to get up and move to the "colored section." When he refused to do so, the private detective arrested him. He was charged with one violation of the Separate Car Act and was remanded to Orleans Parish for trial.

Plessy challenged the law under the Thirteenth and Fourteenth Amendments. He claimed he did not receive "equal treatment under the law." The presiding judge in Orleans Parish ruled that because the railroad operated within the state of Louisiana, they could regulate their company as they saw fit. Plessy was convicted and fined $25. The case was immediately appealed to the Supreme Court of Louisiana.

The Comité des Citoyens provided the lawyers to challenge the Separate Court Act to the Supreme Court of Louisiana. This court decided that the previous judge's ruling had been sound and would stand. The justices declared there had been no violation of the Fourteenth Amendment, as the court was able to cite precedents in a couple of cases in the North. For instance, the Massachusetts Supreme Court had ruled that segregated schools were constitutional. However, this ruling took place in 1849, which was before the ratification of the Fourteenth Amendment. The Louisiana justices also spoke of another case, which came out of Pennsylvania. A law mandated separate railcars for different races, just as the New Orleans law did. In this case, the Pennsylvania Supreme Court said that having segregation in place doesn't mean one is below another. Instead, "it is simply to say that following the order of Divine Providence, human authority ought not to compel these widely separated races to intermix."

Since the Supreme Court of Louisiana failed to issue the ruling the Comité des Citoyens was searching for, the group appealed to the United States Supreme Court. This was the plan all along, as the committee hoped to have segregation declared unconstitutional throughout the entire country.

The Supreme Court agreed to hear the case, and it was added to the docket in 1896. Two separate legal briefs for Plessy were submitted to the court by Albion W. Tourgée and Samuel F. Phillips. Tourgée was considered to be the most outspoken white Republican in the nation on the issue of equality. He was an instrumental member of the Comité des Citoyens; in fact, he was the one to suggest that the man who boarded the train be fairer-skinned. Both gentlemen testified for Plessy at the Supreme Court hearing, although Tourgée played a larger role in the case. They claimed that Plessy had rights under the Thirteenth and Fourteenth Amendments, which were violated by the Separate Car Act. They argued that the Equal Protection Clause guarantees the same rights to all United States citizens. Tourgée also argued that since the reputation of black men was as slaves or property, they were considered to be inferior and given poorer separate accommodations.

Attorney General Milton Joseph Cunningham wrote the state's legal brief. He was known for his efforts to restore white supremacy. In fact, Cunningham worked so vigorously in restoring white supremacy in the South that he was eventually arrested himself for violating laws.

Following these oral arguments, the justices took the case under review. They issued their decision on May 18th, 1896. What had begun as a "test case" (cases that bring clarity to certain laws) came to a resolution almost four years later. By a seven to one vote, the Supreme Court rejected Plessy's arguments and ruled for the defendant. The court upheld the Separate Car Act as constitutional.

Only eight justices took part in this decision because one of the justices, Justice David J. Brewer, had missed the oral arguments due to the death of his daughter and was thus recused from the decision-making process. Justice Henry Billings Brown wrote the majority opinion, which first looked at the Thirteenth Amendment. The Supreme Court decided that this law had not violated it, as the majority of justices interpreted the Thirteenth Amendment as providing the necessary amount of equality to abolish slavery. The Thirteenth Amendment did not bestow any other legal equality.

The Supreme Court opinion then turned toward the arguments around the Fourteenth Amendment and the Equal Protection Clause. This clause says, "nor shall any State...deny to any person within its jurisdiction the equal protection of the laws." The court's decision was that the Fourteenth Amendment, while guaranteeing legal equality, did not intend to ban other types of discrimination. In other words, the amendment did not abolish the differences between the races, and it also did not intend for "a commingling of the races upon terms unsatisfactory to either."

The Supreme Court decided that racial separation laws were well within the purview of the state of Louisiana. The court believed that as long as a law was reasonable and was not intended to oppress another, it would remain legal. However, the real question regarding segregation laws was whether or not the law was reasonable. The court believed that the state should have discretionary authority over what was reasonable.

The Supreme Court rejected the argument that segregation dehumanized the black race, saying, "We consider the underlying fallacy of the plaintiff's argument to consist in the assumption that the enforced separation of the two races stamps the colored race with a badge of inferiority. If this be so, it is not by reason of anything found in the act, but solely because the colored race chooses to put that construction on it." With this move, the US Supreme Court declared that "separate but equal" accommodations were certainly constitutional.

Only one justice dissented from this opinion, and he did so with an elegance and grace that has held up under historical scrutiny. John Marshall Harlan believed that the Louisiana law implied that blacks were inferior. In his eloquent dissent, Harlan wrote, "But in view of the Constitution, in the eye of the law, there is in this country no superior, dominant, ruling class of citizens. There is no caste here. Our Constitution is color-blind, and neither knows nor tolerates classes among citizens. In respect of civil rights, all citizens are equal before the law. The humblest is the peer of the most powerful. The law regards man as man, and takes no account of his surroundings or of his color when his civil rights as guaranteed by the supreme law of the land are involved...Everyone knows that the statute in question had its origin in the purpose, not so much to exclude white people from railroad cars occupied by blacks, as to exclude people of color from coaches occupied by or assigned to white persons...Under the guise of giving equal accommodation for whites and blacks, the law sought to compel the latter to keep to themselves while traveling in railroad passenger coaches. No one would be so wanting in candor as to assert the contrary."

Harlan then proposed that this decision would go down in history as one of the worst decisions the Supreme Court ever made. And Harlan was right. Time and time again, scholars have come to the same conclusion that the *Dred Scott v. Sandford* and the *Plessy v. Ferguson* decisions are at the top of the Supreme Court's worst rulings. This decision in *Plessy v. Ferguson* institutionalized segregation in the South for decades to come.

This Supreme Court decision erased all the positive legislative gains of the Radical Reconstruction era. "Separate but equal" became the doctrine of the land, and future Supreme Court cases only strengthened it.

Everyone knows now that the accommodations offered to people of color in this time period were indeed separate, but they were certainly not equal. One of the most significant impacts was in the realm of public schools. Even before this decision by the Supreme Court, funding for white and black schools was significantly unequal. Black schools were typically old, substandard buildings. They were underfunded, and their supplies and textbooks were old and used. In 1927, the US Supreme Court ruled in *Lum v. Rice* that public schools in Mississippi could completely ban Chinese American children from attending white schools. Since going to school was compulsory, the Supreme Court ruled that Lum could choose to attend a private school or attend schools with other minorities.

When blacks began to migrate again to the North to enjoy more equality, segregation and Jim Crow laws simply followed them. Amusement parks and swimming pools in states like Indiana were whites-only well into the 1950s. Oftentimes in the North, segregation was not the law but rather an unspoken expectation.

Plessy v. Ferguson also allowed states throughout the South to prevent people of color from registering and voting. The state's legislatures put more obstacles in place beyond the literacy tests and poll taxes. For example, some states required one to be a property owner in order to vote.

In 1954, the US Supreme Court in *Brown v. Board of Education* declared that segregation in public schools was not equal and was unconstitutional. *Plessy v. Ferguson* was no longer the precedent on segregation issues, even though it was never explicitly overturned.

Finally, in 1964, the Civil Rights Act outlawed any form of segregation. The Voting Rights Act of 1965 put the federal government back into an oversight and enforcement role with respect to registering and voting.

In 2009, Keith Plessy and Phoebe Ferguson, descendants of the original plaintiff and defendant in the 1896 case, joined together to form the Plessy and Ferguson Foundation for Education and Reconciliation. This foundation aims to teach the true history of the civil rights struggle in the United States. They use art, film, and other public programs to let others understand *Plessy v. Ferguson* and its impact over the years.

For those interested in viewing history firsthand, a marker has been placed at the corner of Press and Royal Streets in Louisiana, recognizing the place where Plessy boarded that whites-only train car all those years ago.

Afterword: The Legacy of Reconstruction and Today's Civil Rights Issues

As we look at the political and social climate in the United States in the early 20th century, we might be fooled into believing that we have left the Civil War and its Reconstruction far behind us. After all, the civil rights movement of the 1960s resulted in new legislation and voting rights. Today, blacks and whites work together, live in the same neighborhoods, and socialize together. On the outside, it appears as if systemic racism is a relic of the past.

However, the year 2020 heard cries from the black community, whose voices were raised, yet again, in the name of social justice and equality. This is a highly contentious topic in the United States today, but it is important to examine why the African American community feels this way, especially as it relates directly to what was set in place during Reconstruction. Blacks continue to outnumber whites in prisons, although the number between the two has been steadily decreasing over the years. And although white people have the highest mortality rate when it comes to police violence, one has to keep in mind that there are more white people than black people in the United States, which means that black people suffer more in this sphere as well. In addition to this, blacks also face worsening voter rights. In 2013, the US Supreme Court struck down two provisions of the Voting Rights Act of 1965, one of which had required local and state governments to obtain federal approval before changing voting laws. Since then, nearly 1,000 polling places have been closed, with the majority of these in predominately African American districts. Many have also felt that stricter voter ID laws and rules regarding mail-in or absentee ballots are symptoms of the same racial disease the country has suffered from since its inception. To be fair, many people believe these types of laws are not racist but are simply intended to prevent voter fraud or to decrease government spending, but it can be hard to determine where the line between the two starts and ends. Regardless of the differences in opinion, there is still a divide in the United States today.

We will leave you with some final questions, questions that scholars are still trying to answer today. Was the Reconstruction successful, or did it only perpetuate systemic racism in the nation? And was there ever really a chance to get beyond the hurt and bitterness caused by the Civil War?

Part 2: The Gilded Age

A Captivating Guide to an Era in American History That Overlaps the Reconstruction Era and Coincides with Parts of the Victorian Era in Britain along with the Belle Époque in France

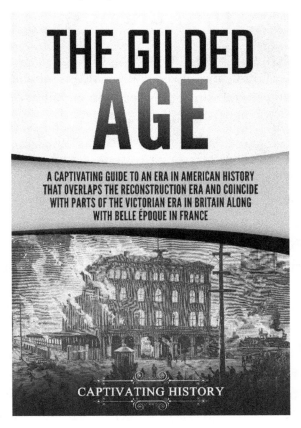

Introduction

From a modern perspective, it may seem that the United States was a major powerhouse since its early days. Its present-day economic, military, and cultural strength gives out an aura of everlasting magnificence, possibly even that it was God-given. That's how some may see it, at least. However, the truth is far from it. The American story started hundreds of years ago when it was a lowly European colony, far from the grandeur and magnificence the world associates with it today. Generations worked hard to gradually transform the humble, dependent colonies into bustling independent states, which were united under a single flag.

This transformation from a weak and relatively poor dominion into a world-class international power was undoubtedly a long process, yet it achieved its peak in the late 19th century. At that time, the US managed to achieve change in many aspects, from economic and social to political and military. This period of growth has become known as the Gilded Age.

Yet despite the magnificence that seeps from the name and the associated images of the rising American giant, this age in US history contains some darker tales. It is enough to mention the repression of various minority groups, which were based on racial, gender, and social divisions. From that perspective, it was also a period of struggle for rights and equality, which adds yet another dimension of change to the Gilded Age.

For, in the end, the underlying subtext of the Gilded Age is that of transformation and change, including both the good and the bad. For that reason, this guide will try to tell the story of how the United States managed to adapt, convert, and reshape into what we associate with it to this day. This is merely an introduction, but it will hopefully be one that sparks your interest in learning more about this topic, not to mention history in general.

Chapter 1 – Building the Foundation

Today, the United States of America is one of the most powerful countries by many standards. Too often, this position is taken for granted, especially since it has been in that position for a relatively long time. But it is important to remember that this was not always the case. The beginning of the American story is much humbler, but it is crucial to learn about it to understand the foundation that was laid before the Gilded Age came about. Only after we understand the basis upon which the country was erected can we truly grasp how it transformed into the giant it is today.

Often the tale of the United States begins when it proclaimed its independence from Britain in 1776. However, it actually started before that. In 1492, Christopher Columbus, serving the Spanish Crown, sailed across the Atlantic Ocean, arriving in the modern-day Bahamas. Within years, he went on several more voyages, sending reports of wealth and prosperity to his superiors in Spain. The age of exploration had begun.

Within a few years, John Cabot sailed under the British flag to what is today known as Newfoundland. With that, the European exploration in North America was on its way. However, it should be noted that prior to the famed explorations and discoveries of the 15th and 16th centuries, the Vikings voyaged roughly to the same place as Cabot around 1000 CE. Nonetheless, their expedition was short-lived, and it was soon forgotten, leaving no major mark on history.

Another interesting fact is that both Columbus and Cabot (originally *Giovanni Caboto*) were both Italian, despite serving foreign rulers. It shows that the Age of Discovery was only possible thanks to the experience of the Italian Renaissance navigators, who had somewhat different views of the world. Soon, other seamen joined the tide, and by the early 16th century, the Europeans started crossing the Atlantic on a regular basis, exploring the coasts of North America. They hailed from various nations, most notably England, France, and Spain. It wasn't long before they realized the land was rich and prosperous. And from their perspective, it was theirs for the taking.

European Colonization as the Bedrock of the US

In modern times, it is usually depicted that the colonization of what is now the United States began in the early 17th century with the arrival of the British Pilgrims at Plymouth Rock. However, this is far from the truth. By the early 1500s, the Spanish explorers began charting the coasts of present-day Florida, and by the 1560s, Spain founded St. Augustine, the first colony in the US.

Mayflower in Plymouth Harbor by William Halsall.
Source: https://commons.wikimedia.org

Farther north, French and British expeditions began discovering the American lands, and it wasn't long before they tried to create colonies of their own. Those initial attempts proved to be failures for various reasons. One of the main ones was the fact the American colonies were far away from their motherlands, making it difficult to resupply and replenish the manpower. However, the French were eventually able to found Quebec City in 1608, while the English formed Jamestown, in what is today Virginia, a year before that.

From these starting points, these three European empires grew. Spain went on to take possession of much of the Southern US, including the territories of Florida, Texas, New Mexico, Arizona, and California. The French swung down from the Great Lakes region, following through the central US along the Mississippi River to the Gulf of Mexico, founding numerous cities, most notably New Orleans. Finally, the British took possession of the eastern coast of the US, creating the famous Thirteen Colonies.

It's worth noting that other nations, most notably the Netherlands and Sweden, formed colonies in the same region as the British. The most notable was New Amsterdam, which was founded by the Dutch in 1624. The Netherlands and Britain broke out into conflict, and by 1664, the latter took control over the city. Soon afterward, it was renamed New York. This implies that from the very beginning of colonization, the lands of the United States were settled by people of various nationalities, not solely the British. Additionally, the expeditions weren't always manned by the nation funding the colonization. For example, the first Polish settlers came to the Jamestown colony in 1608, while Germans were part of both the Dutch and English crews.

That being said, looking at the birth of the United States solely from the eyes of the colonists is misinforming. Although the Europeans saw these lands as free for the taking, there were numerous native tribes living across the US. The relations between the settlers and the natives were complex, to say the least. Jamestown was able to survive because the local indigenous population was willing to trade with the colonists. However, in other cases, the Europeans were sometimes treated as unwelcome invaders. That sentiment soon proved right, as the conflicts between the settlers and the natives increased, as the former was seeking to conquer the native lands. Throughout the 17th and 18th centuries, numerous wars were fought, not only over the control of territories but also because the colonists tended to mistreat the natives.

Apart from the intentional destruction of the native tribes, which slowly retreated in front of the relentless colonists, the indigenous population was also ravaged by the diseases brought by the settlers. Smallpox, measles, and other illnesses that were rarely deadly to the Europeans, as their immune systems were accustomed to it, ravaged the native population. The range of this inadvertent massacre is hard to estimate. Modern historians' lowest approximations are usually around 30 percent, while some go up to 70 percent or even higher. Even though this massacre was unintentional, it was clear the Europeans saw the natives as lesser beings, second-class humans, or even as beasts. Sometimes, they outright killed them, and sometimes they tried to "civilize" them, disregarding their culture in the process. The indigenous people were even enslaved and traded with as common livestock. This kind of treatment became the norm, and later on, it became a part of US politics after the colonies gained their independence.

Apart from Native Americans and European settlers, there was another group that played an important role in the creation of the United States. Those people were Africans, who unfortunately weren't coming to the new continent of their own free will. Bought as slaves and shipped across the Atlantic as private property, the first Africans arrived on the American continent as far back as 1503 when Spanish colonists brought them to work the fields. Other nations soon followed. For instance, the British first brought African slaves to Jamestown in around 1619. Since that time, their numbers grew steadily, and they became an integral part of American life. Modern estimates state that Africans made up as much as 20 percent of the overall population in the British colonies just prior to the American Revolution. The percentages were much higher in the southern territories, where they went up over 50 percent in certain areas.

There were two main reasons why the European colonists brought African slaves to the New World. Firstly, it was an economic decision. The main source of income in the Americas was tobacco and cotton, both of which were rather labor-intensive to produce. To generate more income, the colonists needed a larger workforce and, if possible, a free source of labor to maximize production and profits. Initially, the natives were seen as a possible source of "free" slave labor. However, as the indigenous population quickly started to decrease due to diseases, the Europeans turned to Africans, which was the second reason. Unfortunately, the Europeans saw the African slaves, just as they did the natives, as lesser beings. Thus, they felt little to no remorse in treating them as harshly as they did.

Despite how they were treated, the African slaves, who, after a few generations, became known as African Americans, played a crucial role in forming the United States. Not only did they provide the labor needed for economic growth, but their culture and influences also affected how the US grew and developed. As such, telling any story about the American past without adding their perspective would be faulty and misleading.

Another cornerstone of the colonial foundations was religion. No matter how you look at it, faith played an important role in how US society was formed. The Spaniards brought Catholicism to the Americas, and one of their core tasks was to spread it among the natives. It was part of their rather skewed view of the world, as they felt it was their God-given mission to convert every "savage" to Christianity, thus bringing them civilization. Of course, it goes without saying that this kind of thinking is an equivalent of a cultural massacre, yet it is important not to erase it from our past. The French were also mainly Catholics, and they shared a similar, though possibly less zealous, view about spreading Christianity.

In contrast to them, most of the English settlers were Protestants, for example, the already mentioned Pilgrims, as well as Presbyterians, Quakers, Puritans, and Baptists. Some of them went to the New World to escape religious persecution or to attempt to form new "pure" societies, ones that were removed from the European sins. Alongside them were also Dutch and German Calvinists. Like some of the Spaniards, some members of these groups were also quite zealous, and they saw religion as an important part of their lives. As such, they believed their mission was to convert the native population to Christianity and ensure they adopted their "pure" Protestant lifestyle. The African slaves were also subjected to conversion, both from the Catholics and from the Protestants.

Apart from the religious foundations, another important link in forming the United States was profit. A number of settlements, including Jamestown and New Amsterdam, were founded by private companies seeking ways to earn money. Those businesses were usually backed by the European states, who then went on to take over the control of the colonies. However, the change in who ruled over the American communities didn't transform how they were governed. The British government still held monetary gain above all, imposing taxes and mercantilism politics. Thus, profit and the economy were some of their primary concerns.

On the other hand, it seemed that the newly conquered lands were actually quite rich, offering a lot of possibilities to those who chose to seek fortune in them. The seeds of the idea that with enough hard work and a little bit of luck, anyone could make a decent living in the American colonies was formed. That was enough to attract numbers of poor people from across Europe to move to the colonies, giving additional diversity to the population, both in national and religious terms.

Additionally, the British rule over the Thirteen Colonies was largely lax, leaving them to practically self-govern themselves. This also meant that the traditional European aristocracy largely failed to permeate colonial society. There were wealthy, higher-class settlers, like some of the more notable early Virginians, but their titles and formalities held little sway over social status. The only important factor was one's success and fortune, allowing for considerably easier social mobility.

From a Colony to a Country

Despite the fact that Britain's colonial rule was rather lax, the clashes between European empires often spilled over into their vast dominions. Thus, a number of wars were fought between the colonists in what is today the United States. Although these wars were partly fought by the local population, they were still expensive.

This prompted the British to impose higher taxes, advocating the colonies had to pay for their safety.

Over the several decades of the 18th century, these levies steadily increased, spurring dissatisfaction among the people. To make matters worse, despite paying their dues to the British Crown, American colonists had no political rights in the empire. By 1775, when it was clear no compromise could be achieved, the Thirteen Colonies rebelled against the British. A year later, they declared their independence, promoting the goals of their struggle, which were achieving "certain unalienable Rights, that among these are Life, Liberty and the pursuit of Happiness." These ideals, written down by Thomas Jefferson in the Declaration of Independence and edited by the Second Continental Congress, became the ideological foundation of the United States.

Declaration of Independence by John Trumbull.
Source: https://commons.wikimedia.org

After several years of combat, the war ended in an American victory, and through the Treaty of Paris of 1783, US independence was internationally recognized. Over the next several years, the colonies continued to exist in a loose confederation before the Constitution was drafted in 1787, with Rhodes Island being the last state to approve it in 1790. The Constitution further echoed the ideas and ideals of the Declaration of Independence, indicating that the government should serve its people and placing justice and liberty as the core values of the new states.

However, the enlightened principles on which the US Constitution was based were largely limited in scope. First of all, slavery was still legal, and it was somewhat shielded by the Founding Fathers, as they pledged not to meddle in the Atlantic slave trade. It is worth noting that despite their mild stance toward slavery, the word itself wasn't used directly in the Constitution. This was done so the Southern states would join the Union, as their economies were largely based on slave labor.

Besides the practice of slavery, women lacked any rights, and even adult white men had to be property owners and have a certain yearly revenue to be able to vote. These constrictions changed over the decades, eventually giving all white men suffrage rights as long as they paid taxes, although racial and gender determinants were still existent. The natives also lacked any constitutional rights, as they were still largely seen as uncivilized by most Americans.

Even worse for them was the fact that the newly founded United States continued their expansion westward. Settlers took over their lands, and in the process, both sides engaged in atrocities. The fact that the US bought native lands from France in the famous Louisiana Purchase of 1803 shows that the American government didn't recognize indigenous people as any kind of political faction. In their minds, that purchase secured their rights to colonize those lands, which they saw as empty, as there were almost no European settlers in them.

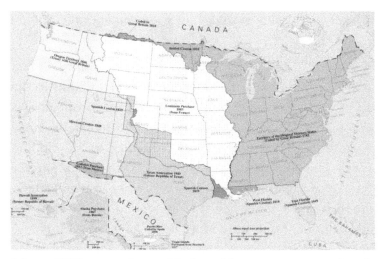

Map of US expansion, with the white area representing the Louisiana Purchase. Source: https://commons.wikimedia.org

The Louisiana Purchase also represented early US policy toward Europe. After securing its independence, America wanted to refrain from meddling in European affairs and keep out major European influences while still maintaining close contacts. However, the US was dragged into a conflict between Britain and France in 1812 over trade. Britain wanted the US to abstain from trading and supplying their enemies. The US refused. After a small naval skirmish over the British blockade of France, the British instigated native attacks on US western borders. America felt it had no choice but to declare war against Great Britain. The war was largely inconclusive and ended in 1814, without any real victories on either side, yet the Americans proclaimed it as their triumph.

The War of 1812 prompted the creation of what was later dubbed the "Monroe Doctrine" in the 1820s. It basically proclaimed the American continent was off limits for further European colonization and meddling. Additionally, it officially proclaimed US neutrality in European affairs. Despite that, the US kept close economic and cultural ties to the old continent. This is most evident through the fact that it was quick to adapt British

Industrial Revolution technology, in some cases improving on their achievements.

The American Industrial Revolution began to slowly manifest in the early days of the nation's independence, but thanks to the War of 1812, it began to pick up speed. Since Britain stopped exporting its goods to the US, Americans were forced to manufacture their own, significantly boosting the investment and development of industries. This industrial proliferation was concentrated in the Northern states, while the Southern ones maintained their agricultural basis. Thus, when the war ended, the South remained an important exporter of cotton to Britain and other parts of Europe, maintaining its economic ties with the old continent.

Cultural ties were no less important, as European culture remained the main influence on the young country. After all, many US citizens still had familial ties that spanned the Atlantic. On top of that, the American elite continued to mimic British fashion and behavior to a certain extent. That was coupled with the constant influx of European migrants, who continued to travel across the ocean in search of better fortunes. With them, they brought some of their customs and traditions, slowly making the US a melting pot of various cultures, from which a more unique American cultural fabric was to be sown.

Religion also continued to play an important role in US society, going through an evangelical revival in the early 19th century. Echoing the ideals of the American Revolution, predeterminism was replaced by the idea of salvation by free will. Throughout these decades, Baptist and Methodist churches gained a substantial number of followers. Additionally, new sects like Mormons and Shakers were also formed; however, these groups challenged traditional values, and they were often persecuted.

Although religious differences between various denominations existed, they didn't interfere with the unity of the young nation, at least not in a significant way. But there were other ways to divide the nation, namely political parties. Two major parties emerged: the Federalists and the Democratic-Republicans.

Federalists, who were led most notably by Alexander Hamilton, argued for a strong federal government, federal taxation, and the overall centralization of the United States. The Federalist Party was also more sympathetic toward the wealthier classes, most notably industrialists, as they saw them as the backbone of economic advancement. With that, they inherently were more oriented toward urban development.

Their opposition was the Democratic-Republican Party, which was led in its early days by Thomas Jefferson. Their political stance was more oriented toward republicanism in the form of a weaker central government. They believed in lesser taxation and were more inclined toward personal freedoms and equality. Unlike the Federalists, they were more in favor of agrarianism and social parity. As such, the Democratic-Republicans were more connected to the rural areas. Another notable difference between the two parties was their stance on foreign policies. The Democratic-Republicans were the pioneers of ideas like expansionism and took a harsher stand toward the British, as they saw them as the most direct threat to the US. In contrast, the Federalists were inclined toward keeping closer trading ties with Europe.

Those differences also exhibited themselves geographically. The Federalists were stronger in the North, as the urban industrial centers saw a centralized state as a beneficial way to expand their business. On the other hand, Democratic-Republicans were largely supported in the South, where most of the large landowners were based. Thus, from its early days, the United States saw the rise of its two-party political system, although it's worth mentioning that the Constitution never stipulated the number of political parties in the US.

Division and War

The United States continued its polarization, both in political and social aspects, while still pushing its geographical and economic growth and development as it approached the mid-19th century. As decades passed, it was clear that the growing friction between the two sides of America was headed toward an explosive resolution.

At first, it seemed that the US would remain united, at least politically. After the War of 1812, the Federalist Party fell apart. Federalists opposed the war, despite the wide public support for the conflict, which led to their downfall. The Democratic-Republican Party remained the sole large party in the nation. However, the party quickly began to fracture, and by the late 1820s, two opposed groups once again formed.

One of the factions of the Democratic-Republican Party formed the Democratic Party, which was led by Andrew Jackson. They continued to favor the agrarian economy, opposed taxes and a central bank, and favored the presidency as the primary governmental branch. In general, they were opposed to a strong and active federal government. Additionally, they were rather against various kinds of reforms, such as public education. Their base of power was mostly in the Southern and frontier states.

Their opposition was the Whig Party, which was under the helm of Henry Clay. This party favored Congress as the main governmental branch, and it sought modernization and economic protection to foster the growth of industry. They sought to achieve this through a more proactive and enterprising rule from Washington, using federal taxes to finance the growth. The Whigs also leaned more toward humanitarian and social reforms. The Northern industrialized states were their main source of political support.

While the major political parties were focused on matters of the economy and government, a new antislavery movement began spreading in the industrial North. They offered several solutions to help address the issue, including returning the slaves back to Africa, engaging in the gradual emancipation of slaves, or the more extreme immediate abolition. This prompted a strong reaction in the Southern states, which saw it as a direct attack on its way of life and income. To defend their positions, Southerners argued that slavery was good for the economy, society, and the culture of the entire US, including the slaves, basing their faulty ideas on their interpretation of history, religion, the economy, legality, and many other justifications.

In contrast, Northerners saw slavery as, above all, an infringement on the ideas of freedom upon which the United States was built, while also as an immoral act that was against the core Christian faith. The racial issue began to tear the unity of the entire nation apart, even when it came to religion. Methodists and Baptists split into Northern and Southern denominations. Some religions were more heavily engaged in supporting antislavery, like, for example, the Quakers, while others were more directly in favor of slavery or ignored the issue, like the Lutherans and Catholics. Both political parties also started to get torn apart over the matter of slavery, as their members began taking sides.

This was a period of marked contrasts within a country that was still being put together, as the division spread further than just the issue of slavery. Since the 1820s, the fabled Wild West was in the process of being "conquered." Through the ideas expressed in the famous Manifest Destiny, the majority of Americans felt ordained to spread across the continent. During this expansion, the settlers continued to expulse the Native Americans from their lands. This was usually done through brute force and wars, as well as forced negotiations, in which the government would resettle tribes to make room for the settlers. During these decades, the US gained more states.

However, the indigenous people weren't the only ones in the US crosshairs. In the mid-1830s, a number of American people moved to Texas, which was, at the time, a part of Mexico. When Mexico banned slavery, those settlers decided to declare independence, causing a violent reaction from Mexico. After some deliberation, Texas was incorporated into the US in 1845. This triggered a war between the United States and Mexico, which lasted from 1846 to 1848. In it, the US gained not only Texas but also California; the region that would become Utah, Nevada, and Colorado; half of the future New Mexico; and most of Arizona.

An illustration depicting a battle from the Civil War.
Source: https://commons.wikimedia.org

Expansionism and conflict were favored by the Democrats, including the forcible resettling of the natives. In contrast, the Whigs opposed these causes, which caused the party to finally fall apart. It was replaced by the Republican Party, which continued with most of the Whig policies, although it added a more pronounced opposition to slavery.

North vs. South

The separate circumstances surrounding the diverse development of the country's regions created different attitudes toward social and political views.

States such as Massachusetts, Connecticut, Rhode Island, New Hampshire, Maine, New Jersey, and Vermont had a skilled, mostly white labor class, a large middle class, and a relatively conservative group of very rich industrialists and entrepreneurs. A slave workforce was practically unheard of in the North. In fact, it was illegal to own slaves in many of these states. They were called the Yankees by Southerners. On the other hand, the Southern states' working force was mostly made up of slaves, with nine out of ten being of African descent. Southerners' wealth was heavily based on this "asset," which was basically free manpower. Hence, there was a contrast between the origins of the upper classes' prosperity in the South compared to their neighbors in the North.

Most of the representatives from the Northern states, with a large majority of them belonging to the Republican Party, were firmly against the existence of slavery as a legal institution in the United States. Their counterparts, who were mostly from the Democratic Party, which represented most of the Southern states, wished to uphold slavery and were against many of the capitalist practices already in place in the North.

Discussions regarding these subjects became more intense in the months preceding the start of the Civil War. Due to a split in the Democratic Party, Republican candidate Abraham Lincoln won the 1860 presidential election, allowing him to pursue his abolitionist policies.

A picture of escaped slaves with Union soldiers.
Source: https://commons.wikimedia.org

This situation put the Southern states—Florida, Tennessee, South and North Carolina, Virginia, Texas, Arkansas, Louisiana, Mississippi, Alabama, and Georgia—against the ropes. These states believed it was only a matter of time before Washington would ban slavery, destroying their economy and way of life. The war seemed inevitable, despite the cost in human lives and destruction. So, they made a radical decision: to separate themselves from the Union and create a new country, the Confederate States of America, with the former Mississippian senator and hero of the Mexican-American War, Jefferson Davis, as their president. The American Civil War ensued, lasting from 1861 to 1865.

During the war, Lincoln and the Union continued their abolitionist program. First, he issued the Emancipation Proclamation in 1862, liberating the slaves in the rebelling states. Then several Republican congressmen proposed the now-famous Thirteenth Amendment in late 1863. Grueling Congress sessions endlessly discussed the approval of this amendment, which stated that "neither slavery nor involuntary servitude, except as a punishment for crime whereof the party shall have been duly convicted, shall exist within the United States, or any place subject to their jurisdiction." Despite Republicans having the clear supremacy in Congress, the amendment was passed more than a year later, on January 31st, 1865, effectively marking the end of slavery in the US.

Simultaneously with the political struggle against servitude, the fight against it on the battlefield also raged on. After four exhausting, cruel, and deadly years, calculations put the death toll at more than 200,000 souls and more than 400,000 wounded between both sides. The destruction and damage to infrastructure were also high. Nonetheless, the North eventually prevailed. After the Confederacy dissolved itself, there was not much for the Southerners to do. They had lost the war, and thankfully, their battle for slavery as well.

From Ruins to the Gilded Age

After the end of the American Civil War, the majority of the US was in shambles, and there was much to be rebuilt and a whole lot more to build anew. The semi-industrialized North and the more agrarian South started to be radically reshaped after this terrible conflict, which killed thousands and ripped apart the still-emerging country.

The losses on both sides were terrible. Roughly 2 percent of the US population died. However, even with the Civil War deaths, by 1870, the population was already on the rebound, with more than thirty-eight million inhabitants, which was a whopping 22.6 percent increase with regard to 1860 statistics. By the end of the century, the American population had already surpassed seventy-six million, becoming one of the most populous countries on Earth. This was an impressive growth rate, taking into account that barely one hundred years before—in 1800—the US population was only five million.

At this point, the country started receiving a whole new set of settlers, who came from various parts of the world. Until then, American immigrants had mostly come from Northern Europe.

This would change after the end of the Civil War. For example, many Asians started arriving in the Pacific Ocean ports, and they settled in many western areas, with San Francisco as a particularly favorite site. However, 70 percent of the newer immigrants came through New York and its now-famous Staten Island, where everyone coming in had to pass through.

People from other parts of Europe joined the "itch" to come to America, like the Italians, Irish, Poles, Bulgarians, and Hungarians, as well as from lands beyond the European continent, such as Lebanon, Syria, Palestine, Jordan, and other areas from the Ottoman Empire. These Arab immigrants to the United States were a mix of Christian and Muslim groups. Most of them preferred to settle in large cities, although a considerable portion went to booming Midwestern towns, such as Pittsburgh, Detroit, and Michigan City. They were attracted by the wide range of flourishing factories there, as the Industrial Revolution in the US soon began to pick up speed.

The melting pot was getting very rich. Nearly twelve million immigrants arrived in the United States between 1870 and 1900. All came looking for jobs—and there was plenty, although the lifestyle was not for everyone. Many immigrants were highly exploited, earning meager wages and working long hours. But the dream was still there. Getting to America was the objective, and many of those workers managed to start a new life with their families.

The United States became admired for its economic possibilities, vast stretches of cheap land, and its increased grandiosity in everything they built, which firmly took hold during the Gilded Age. Private houses and gardens were famous for being extremely large, railroad projects covered thousands of miles all over the country, and US hotels were sumptuous, with gigantic rooms, "modern" bathrooms, and luxury settings. Just to give an example of the differences between American and European accommodations, by 1858, the Continental Hotel in Philadelphia was able to provide lodging for 800 to 900 visitors, while the largest European hotel, the Queens Hotel in Cheltenham, England — "the most grandiose hotel in Europe"—only had 110 rooms. Europeans started embracing the idea of having magnificent hotels so much that they received the first complaint of "Yankee cultural colonization," with French writer Edmond de Goncourt grieving in 1870 that Paris hotels were becoming "Americanized."

Despite the advancements the US had made, the western part of the nation was still not united as a whole. There were large areas that were not even a part of the United States. After the Civil War, peace came, along with the quest to unite this entire stretch of land into one giant nation. This set the wheels in motion for a titanic railroad project that persistently forged its way west. The project came with a wide range of benefits but also rearranged many people's lives.

The potential benefits of connecting the East and the West through a railroad system were recognized in an 1852 report to the US Congress, which stated that "we can move property upon railroads at the rate of 15 cents per ton per mile, or for one-tenth the cost upon the ordinary road." The eventual cost-cutting benefits of transporting all kinds of goods would be astounding indeed. Thanks to the expanding railroad, the US economy started booming. The iron and steel industries exploded, and cheaper and faster transport expanded trade. With that came the ideals of a consumer economy and cheaper mass-produced goods. By the 1870s, the so-called Gilded Age had begun, erupting from the numerous changes in US society, economy, and culture.

But why did this American period receive the nickname of the Gilded Age? The name that was coined to identify the approximate forty years of prosperity in the US came from none other than the title of Mark Twain's first novel, *The Gilded Age*, which was co-authored with Charles Dudley Warner. This novel made its mark due to its sharp criticism of how the different government and business powers worked at the time, as they were filled with corruption and hypocrisy. The novel also reveals a stark outlook on the social inequalities during this part of 19th-century America, with its grow-rich-fast businessmen showing off their newfound wealth alongside a huge mass of impoverished farmers and workers.

This period of American history is fascinating in all its glory and misery. We can accurately argue that the Gilded Age set the stage for the final unification of the nation as we know it today, with each of its fifty states bringing its own distinct quality to the table. Their integration brought much diversity yet also a distinct unity among those who call themselves "Americans."

Chapter 2 – From Chaos to the Gilded Age

Since its independence, the United States adopted many of the economic, social, and political innovations that were going on in Europe, particularly in England. Yet not all of the areas within the US developed in the same way. The Northern states became industrialized much faster than the Southern states, which had adopted an economic structure based on agriculture, with cotton and tobacco crops being especially important. These staples brought much wealth and comprised a large percentage of the US exports back then. Additionally, Southern states were primarily food producers, chiefly growing wheat and rice.

By the time of the Civil War, the North had over 100,000 factories, with more than a million workers, while in the South, there were only around 20,000 factories, which hired a little over 100,000 workers. So, in the early years after the country's independence, the Northern states mostly provided for finished goods, while the Southern ones mainly delivered food staples. Nevertheless, this relative synergy between the North and South deteriorated throughout the 19th century.

Though slavery was the central issue that caused division between Northern and Southern states, many political and social issues were carried across the borders. A majority of these were based upon their differences in the basic economic structure. These were only exaggerated by the destruction of the Civil War, which caused even greater disparities and shook the foundations of the South's economy and politics. These issues had to be addressed so the United States could continue its growth.

A Spectacular New Opportunity

The conflict brought inevitable destruction. The economy was left in shambles, and much of the infrastructure—especially that of the states in which most of the battles occurred, such as Virginia, Kentucky, and Tennessee—was destroyed. Large groups of people, especially former slaves for obvious reasons, farmers, and immigrants, started migrating to different parts of the country—not only from the South to the North but also toward the large expanses of lands to the west, which held much promise.

The end of the Civil War marked a new beginning for the ravaged nation. A decisive group of leaders decided to set innovative ideas in motion so the country could reinvent itself. The somewhat chaotic state of affairs during the post-war years was the perfect opportunity for the United States to rethink many aspects of its structure—socially, economically, and geographically. Some ideas flourished, while others failed resoundingly, yet the results were positive in the long run. They managed to place the US as an emerging world power by the turn of the century, and some actions taken during the post-war years were key to this development.

The Reconstruction Acts, which were passed in both 1867 and 1868, were crucial for rebuilding the country. Abraham Lincoln had been elected to another term, but he was brutally killed less than two months into his second term as president. Lincoln did not even live to see the final approval of those ideas he had fought so much for, as he died about a week after the Civil War ended. His successor, Andrew Johnson, who presided over the complex Reconstruction process.

Despite the name, the Reconstruction Acts weren't tied to rebuilding devastated lands and the economy. In fact, their main goal was aimed at political and social reconstruction. Many aspects of these acts were related to the inclusion of former slaves as citizens in their own right. US Congress passed the Thirteenth Amendment on January 31st, 1865, and it was ratified on December 6th, 1865, thus abolishing slavery once and for all within all the states of the Union.

An illustration of freedmen voting in New Orleans in 1867.
Source: https://commons.wikimedia.org

The Fourteenth Amendment was ratified in 1868. It demanded "equal protection of the laws," which included over four million former slaves. The Fifteenth Amendment was the last Reconstruction amendment, and it was ratified in 1870. This amendment stated that all US citizens would be granted the right to vote, regardless of race and previous servitude. This act was mainly aimed at recently liberated African American slaves, giving hope that all those living within the United States would one day be equal under federal law, at least concerning men. The fight for women's suffrage would start during this period of American history, although it would not be until 1920 that this right would become law.

Some regions still insisted on implementing separate rights for blacks and whites, so the country imposed the requirement that each state requesting to be readmitted into the Union had to accept the Fourteenth Amendment.

Thanks to the Military Acts of 1867 and 1868, the federal government, which was still under tight Republican rule, used military presence in the Southern states to enforce these amendments, as well as other acts and laws that had been passed after the end of the war. Tennessee was exempted from this "occupation," as it had already ratified the Fourteenth Amendment, but the other ten states were divided into five military districts. The US Army and its commanding offices were authorized to keep order and protect the people and property. These states were basically under martial law.

Under strict federal guidance, the Confederate states ratified these amendments, achieving the conditions set by Washington for their official rejoining into the United States. By July 1870, with the readmission of Georgia, the United States was whole again. Despite forcing the Reconstruction amendments on the Southern states, some of the states that didn't fight on the Confederate side wouldn't pass them for a long time. Most ironically, Kentucky, the home state of Abraham Lincoln, ratified these amendments as late as 1976.

Despite laws being passed and enforced by the Northern military, racism remained strong. Devastated by the war and poverty, many of the Southern whites blamed the black population for their misery. Riots ensued, with white mobs attacking African Americans in Memphis and New Orleans in 1866. Alongside the hated African Americans, the rioters blamed the "damn Yankees" for their troubles as well.

The military tried to prevent these outbursts, yet that very same year, the infamous Ku Klux Klan started to spread across several Confederate states. The US government tried to suppress their actions both by law and by force, yet the KKK continued to harass both the black population as well as the whites who supported them publicly. In the end, the KKK proved to be beyond the reaches of the law, as it was protected by the connections some of the higher members had. This so-called "social club" continued its terroristic agenda far into the 20th century, and its presence is still felt in the US today.

Racism wasn't something limited to the former slave-owning society of the Southern states. Although many Northerners didn't support slavery as a concept, they had plenty of demeaning opinions about African Americans. Some saw them as lazy or unable to learn or do complicated tasks, among other similar belittling beliefs. Thus, the problem of racial injustice was more widespread and too deeply rooted in the social fabric of the United States to be quickly solved by a war and three amendments.

During the Reconstruction period, the government and some of the Republican leaders tried to combat these prejudices and inequalities by politically activating the newly freed black population, by opening schools for them, and by giving out some form of economic aid. Though these actions provided some relief to the African American population in the South, their position still remained rather hard.

Many of the freed slaves were given nothing more than just their freedom, making them basically the poorest social group in the country. Since they usually lacked any education or skilled training, most of the freed blacks basically returned to the plantations they had once labored on to work for miserably low wages. Some managed to gather funds and began migrating to other states, where they hoped to escape the constant bullying and oppression.

As the years passed, the Republican North grew tired of the struggles in the Southern states and became more enticed by other issues, such as those concerning the economy. The military control over the South began to ease up before the Reconstruction era finally finished in 1877. The Southern states were left to govern themselves as the federal government's focus shifted to other issues. Many hoped that after more than ten years of tight federal rule, the Southern societies had changed enough for some kind of justice to exist.

That kind of faith proved to be misplaced. In a matter of years, the Southern states began to infringe on the rights of the black population. The Jim Crow laws were passed from state to state, enforcing legal segregation in public facilities and transport. The crooked notion of "equal but separate" permeated these laws. What was even worse in the long run was the political disenfranchisement African Americans faced. Many of the Southern states passed discriminatory laws that made voting harder to accomplish for minorities, such as poll taxes, literacy and comprehension tests, and residency requirements. As a result, many African Americans lost their political rights, accompanied by a minority of poor whites.

These discriminatory laws also spread in other states, although they didn't infringe on African American voting rights. They were more concerned with public separation and the ban on interracial marriage. In the end, the Jim Crow laws, which continued to get passed and enforced until the mid-20th century, brought about the backdoor institutionalization of political, social, economic, and educational disadvantages, which affected the Southern black population the most.

Though racial inequality was more than present, the fact remains that in the aftermath of the Civil War, African Americans gained a plethora of new opportunities that most had lacked in previous years. They gained their freedom, tens of thousands acquired some level of education, some managed to build various careers, and the ones with the most stubbornness and willingness to persist managed to build respectable careers in politics, academics, and other similar high-class positions.

Nevertheless, African Americans would still have another century of struggle ahead to achieve full equality and desegregation, especially in the Southern states, where separate schools, places on the bus (remember Rosa Parks), bathrooms, and even water fountains stayed in place until well into the mid-1960s. However, their fight for full social justice still hasn't been fulfilled, and their struggle continues to this day.

Blossoming of the Economy and Industry

The Civil War left the country ravaged, indebted, and economically ruined. The prosperity of the United States became questionable. Southern exports of cotton and tobacco were hindered by the lower production rates since slavery had been banished, and the Northern war efforts drained the budget. So, while the country was going through a political reconstruction, the economy was reviving itself.

The sheer speed of the country's economic recovery was astounding. Firstly, the US had a lot of natural resources, like various minerals, vast forests, and large rivers. Combined with that, the United States also had a surge in population, both from natural reproduction and immigration. This made labor cheap, which was necessary for an economic boom. Finally, a number of innovators, both in the US itself and in Europe, continued to develop technologies that made mass production easier and more efficient. Through laborsaving machinery, US production simply skyrocketed.

However, these factors could only help grow the economy so much. Beyond that, the government had to intervene. The nation began protecting homegrown businesses by introducing tariffs and offering subsidies for companies that would invest in future developments of the infrastructure, like the railroads. To compensate for the drop in agricultural production in the South, a number of Homestead Acts were passed. The first one was approved during the Civil War in 1862, and through it, the federal government began distributing free 160-acre parcels for citizens to farm. Here, the economy proved a stronger force than social norms, as these lots were even given to women and freed slaves.

Beyond that, the government did one last thing to help the booming economy. Well, actually, the government didn't do; instead, it refused to regulate growing businesses. All the activities, working conditions, and practices of businesses were left unchecked. This allowed the formation of unencumbered anarchic capitalism, free of income taxes, regulations, and other kinds of entrepreneurial hindering. It helped the growth of the economy, but it also meant the workers and the environment could be mercilessly exploited, and it allowed corruption to become rampant. Large businesses started meddling in politics as well, ensuring that this kind of fertile atmosphere remained untethered.

The marriage of politicians and wealthy businessmen permeated much of the Gilded Age. Politicians did all in their power to make the rich even richer, while the richer gave some of the spoils and their influence in return. Thus, the late 19th century had a substantial number of affairs and scandals, yet those did little to cause major change.

A caricature depicting wealthy industrialists being carried by their workers. Source: https://commons.wikimedia.org

However, as the century began to come to a close, initial steps to cut corruption were made. Anti-monopoly laws were passed, and a merit system for awarding governmental jobs and positions replaced the old practice of political favors. Corruption remained an issue, but by the end of the century, the first steps toward solving the issue were made.

While the wealthy and the politicians continued to amass money and power, the lower classes reaped some benefits from the bustling economy. The working class was indeed exploited, working long hours in terrible conditions for miserable pay. Yet thanks to the advancements in industrial manufacturing, the costs of living started to drop. That kind of development meant that from 1860 to 1890, real wages grew by about 50 percent. Even the lower classes were living better than before.

It seemed that everyone, including the freed slaves, was benefiting from the booming economy. There was an abundance of jobs and opportunities, and everyone was trying to achieve what was to become known as the American Dream. However, one group suffered immensely, at least partially because of that developing economy: the Native Americans.

As industry and agriculture needed more raw materials and farmable lands, the frontier of the United States continued to expand westward. The indigenous population, what remained of it by that point, stood in the way of that prosperity and progress. The Native Americans just wanted to keep their way of life, to hunt buffalo and live off the land that the US so greatly coveted. As the frontiersmen continued to wash upon them, the Native Americans began pushing back, giving the government a perfect excuse to lead wars against them.

After a series of local wars, battles, and skirmishes, the indigenous population was shattered. By 1890, the year of the famous Wounded Knee massacre, the last notable resistance of the Native Americans was extinguished. Over the decades, what remained of the native population was gathered in reservations that had been allotted to the tribes by the federal government.

Though this may sound like an act of salvation, it rarely was. Most of these reservations consisted of less farmable land and lessened the expenses of the state. It was cheaper to house and feed the native population than to continue fighting them. The indigenous tribes often continued to be plagued by illness and famine, which only helped to continue their population decline. On top of that, throughout the second half of the 19th century, US politicians decided that "Americanizing" the natives was the only way for them to become part of "civilized society," causing a tremendous cultural massacre as well.

Since those atrocities happened on the frontiers, far from sight and mind of average Americans, not many cared. To many, the only important things were money and the continued economic growth and expansion. However, the Gilded Age soon proved that an unregulated economy might soar high, but it could also crash and burn. Over the next couple of decades, the bubble inflated until it burst in 1893 when numerous railroad companies and banks declared bankruptcy. The US economy plummeted, and unemployment rose, which was followed by social unrest. Though the situation gradually improved, the US entered the 20th century still recovering from the shock of this economic depression.

Why Is It Gilded?

After suffering from war, economic disaster, and the trauma of a torn country, Americans were excited about the future ahead of them. People experienced high hopes for a new era of prosperity during those post-Civil War years. Everyone—whites, blacks, mixed-race, and an increased influx of immigrants from all parts of the world—was intent on "becoming rich," of finding the latest and most innovative road to wealth. The opportunities were many, but there were inevitable possibilities for complete and disastrous failures as well.

A whole new group of what the French called the "nouveau riche," or "newly rich," started springing up. And they wanted to flaunt their wealth to everyone around them. They wanted everything bigger, shinier, and as sumptuous as possible. This very flashy way to show off how prosperous one was became the key to this era's nickname—the Gilded Age.

As mentioned above, Mark Twain, the famous American author, titled his first novel *The Gilded Age,* and the phrase was used to describe the atmosphere of opulence and corruption within the United States. Even though it is not his most well-known or best work, it became the foremost reference for those wishing to capture the raw essence of this era, which was filled with faltering progress, big business and big failures, greed, and political corruption. Twain and his co-author sharply criticized both the congressional as well as the judicial systems. There was not a sector of society that escaped their scathing writing—politicians, those get-rich-quick entrepreneurs, journalists, and society in general were all caricatured in this tale.

One of the main characters in *The Gilded Age* is "Colonel" Beriah Sellers, an amiable man who places all of his efforts into getting rich, calling himself "a businessman." However, he wants this money to be fast and easy. Twain constructs a series of satirical situations involving Sanders in many comical circumstances. Throughout the novel, the author intertwines the colonel's path to desired wealth with those of corrupt men, who were willing to buy their seats into Congress or even murder in order to achieve their goals. There is also intense love and deep betrayal, a whole lot of speculators, and many magnificent economic deals gone bad.

Mark Twain (1871) and the cover of The Gilded Age.
Source: https://commons.wikimedia.org

Mark Twain's novel not only set the name for this period in American history, but it also set the standard for mixing fiction and social critique in a unique satirical style. Other books, as well as plays and other diverse intellectual works, followed Twain's style. In sum, the political novels of the Gilded Age represent the beginning of a new strain in American literature: fiction as a vehicle for social protest.

But what does "gilded" exactly mean? Why was it not called a "Golden Age," a common term used for moments in history where real accomplishments were attained? Seventeenth-century Spain, for example, was called "the Golden Century" because some of the best writers of all time, such as Miguel de Cervantes, Calderón de la Barca, and Luis de Góngora, lived during that era. Something gilded is not really made of gold; it is only gold-coated, meaning it is not the "real thing." It is just embellished to make something look expensive, and for some, it was a perfect allegory for this period in American history.

It is easy to demonize America's Gilded Age as one of corruption, greed, and decadent capitalism, yet it was a crucial formative period in the country's history. The Gilded Age was when the US started its transformation into a truly modern society. This society would have been more akin to today's industrial setup, which was a change from its former bucolic agrarian society that had characterized much of its structure in both pre- and post-independence years. Thus, the only way to fully understand this formative period of the United States is to recognize both its good and bad sides, embracing the meaning of gilded.

Chapter 3 – Economic Boom and Bust

Between 1870 and 1900, America was ripe for a gigantic wave of entrepreneurship projects and grandiose economic expansion. However, the US also proved to be fertile ground for the lack of scruples, deceit, and misconduct, which tainted many of the good deeds of this time.

The Robber Barons

In *The Gilded Age*, Mark Twain and Charles Dudley Warner portray some of the wildly rich American tycoons of the latter part of the 19th century, writing on "the manufacture of giant schemes, of speculation of all sorts [and of] inflamed desire for sudden wealth." In many ways, this characterization is true to many of the robber barons' lives and ways. The term "robber baron" stems from medieval times. Back then, it was common for feudal lords—many of them with the title of baron—to rob merchants and travelers that passed through their domains. American newspapers in the 19th century started using this term to describe highly successful businessmen. These men were mostly regarded as capitalists who had, in many instances, become monopolists.

The term stuck, and it wasn't completely untrue. Many of these industrialists amassed their fortunes based only on crass financial speculation and outright fraud or by cheating the stockholders of the companies they had built.

A caricature depicting the robber barons dividing the lands.
Source: https://commons.wikimedia.org

Such was the case of Jay Gould and James Fisk, two cunning men who built a large capital basically through extortion, market manipulation, and even by trying to bribe America's president at the time, General Ulysses S. Grant. Both managed to avoid paying for their financial crimes, even though their speculation with the gold market severely harmed the country's economy for a few months; many gold investors lost everything because of them. These scheming manipulations were the ones that most inspired Twain and Warner.

Other similar magnates were shipping and railroad tycoon Cornelius Vanderbilt, who was the first person to be called a "robber baron" in an 1859 *New York Times* article; Andrew

Carnegie, an implacable man who made a fortune based on the steel industry; and investment banker John Pierpont (J. P.) Morgan, who also invested heavily in the railroad business. It is also impossible not to mention John D. Rockefeller, an oil tycoon who was, at one point, the richest man alive.

Although it is easy to cast disparagements on these men and their unscrupulous methods, the real story is not that simple. Although they might have engaged in crooked dealings, many of these millionaires were highly efficient entrepreneurs who brought a whole new range of products and services to the American people. Many of these visionary men set the basis for America's modern industrial economy, implementing new managerial practices and shifting the view from small companies to big corporations, many of which would eventually become transnational enterprises.

These tycoons invested heavily in new transportation and communication systems. For example, the electrical telegraph—developed between the 1830s and 1840s by American inventor Samuel Morse together with other scientists—became more widespread. Approximately two dozen companies set their efforts on developing this important messaging method, alongside the railroad tracks that were being built across the country. By 1861, the telegraph had already reached California. Other communication technologies were also developed, such as the telephone, the phonograph, and the radio, some of which still exist in our time.

The view of the robber barons, like many other things during the Gilded Age, was twofold. In a positivist view, they helped to develop the industry and the economy, making life better and easier for the masses with their new industrial products and services. Their contribution to American life in this regard cannot be ignored nor downplayed. All of them performed a role in creating the modern way of American life.

In contrast, the negativist view depicts them as ruthless men who were prepared to do morally dubious things for profit, such as exploiting common workers or pulling the strings of corrupt politicians. The businesses began reversing all their positive effects once they turned into untouchable monopolies, as eventually, their greed for power and wealth put their own needs above the wellbeing of the entire nation. Though harsh, this assessment also rings true.

This small group of men, who dominated a great part of America's economy during the second half of the 19th century, provided a sense of prosperity for the whole country, as well as innovation and a culture of being "self-made" people who could succeed in life if provided the opportunity.

The fact is these magnates were, and to a large degree still are, poster examples of capitalism in both its best and worst forms at the same time. Thus, it is hard to correctly assess if they should be seen as a positive or negative force in history. Some may praise them, some may berate them, yet one thing remains certain—their mark on the history of the United States is utterly immeasurable.

Connecting the Nation: The Expansion of the Railroads

One of the key facets of the US economic boom in the late 19th century was the spreading of the railroad. Initial lines, which connected local settlements, spawned as early as the late 1820s, just little more than a decade after the British had developed this technology. Both the entrepreneurs and the government realized the importance of this new form of transportation, and they invested heavily in its development. By the 1850s, this joint effort brought the total length of the railroad system to around 9,000 miles (14,000 kilometers). At that moment, the first magnates, such as Cornelius Vanderbilt and Jay Gould, took a closer interest in this developing branch of industry, prompting an even faster expansion.

However, the United States wasn't yet interconnected by the railway. After a lot of political debate, the Pacific Railroad Acts of 1862 was passed, plotting the first intercontinental line that was to connect the East and the West. After years of hard work, which was usually done by the Chinese workers of the Central Pacific Railroad going eastward and the Irish workers of the Union Pacific Railroad pushing westward, the First Transcontinental Railroad was finished in 1869. It was then possible to travel from New York to San Francisco in just six days, which was unprecedented at that time.

The railroad craze was at its heights, with numerous railway companies popping up and with thousands of people investing in what seemed to be a foolproof business. Between 1868 and 1873, approximately 33,000 miles (53,000 kilometers) of new tracks were laid across the nation, while the accumulated railway network achieved a total length of about 54,000 miles (87,000 kilometers) by 1870. It was an investment that guaranteed a substantial turnover of money.

Photograph of the Transcontinental Railroad's final spike being driven in 1869. Source: https://commons.wikimedia.org

However, their fortunes were to turn quickly. In 1871, Germany decided to stop minting silver coins, which affected the global value of silver. The devaluation of silver prompted the United States government to pass the Coinage Act of 1873, which saw a move from the silver and gold monetary standard to only the gold standard. This meant the worth of the US dollar was now exclusively based on the federal gold reserves.

The federal monetary system was shaken, and people began losing their trust in long-term investments since the domestic monetary supply was reduced. Furthermore, due to less money being in circulation, debts and interests began to rise. By September 1873, Jay Cooke & Company, a prestigious bank and a major railroad investor, went bankrupt. It couldn't pay back its own investors, but it could sell enough Northern Pacific Railroad bonds to cover its expenses.

This prompted a nationwide panic, as many rushed to sell their railroad bonds with banks being unable to cash them out. As a result, dozens of banks and railroad companies went bankrupt, causing a nationwide depression that hit other branches of industry as well as the agriculture sector. Unemployment soared, reaching more than 8 percent by 1878.

The expansion of the railways bogged down, reaching only 1,600 miles (2,600 kilometers) of newly laid tracks in 1875. Even worse for the railroad companies, at least to those that were still operational, were worker strikes. The worst was the so-called Great Railroad Strike of 1877, which started in West Virginia after the Baltimore and Ohio Railroad cut the wages of their workers for the third time in roughly six months. The rebellion spread like wildfire across numerous cities, from New York to St. Louis and Chicago. As the protests became increasingly violent, the newly appointed president, Rutherford B. Hayes, sent the National Guard across the US to suppress the unrest, ending the strike after almost two months.

Labor strikes in the railroad industry continued into the 1880s, yet the overall economic situation began to improve by then. The railway companies reconsolidated, allowing another wave of expansion to begin. A major force behind this revival of the railroad industry was the famous New York financier J. P. Morgan. Over the decade, he restructured several railroad companies, reducing speculations and increasing efficiency. However, his ultimate goal was to form an integrated rail system.

To achieve that, Morgan organized several conferences in 1889 and 1890, which involved numerous railroad presidents and owners. In these meetings, the transportation barons agreed upon a business standard, including prices. By eliminating the competition between companies, Morgan created a railway monopoly, which could keep the prices high. The government reacted by passing an anti-monopoly law known as the Sherman Antitrust Act of 1890, which tried to regulate competition between businesses.

By the early 1890s, railroad companies were once again booming, with tens of thousands of miles of new tracks being laid. The industry was nearing overproduction based on unreliable investments. Unfortunately for the railroad stock owners, an international economic crisis hit in 1893.

Known as the Panic of 1893, this crisis was triggered by the bankruptcy of the Philadelphia and Reading Railroad, one of the largest companies in the US at the time. Panic began spreading across the country, which was further fueled by the similar economic disasters that sprawled up in Europe. Then another large business, the National Cordage Company, failed as well, triggering a domino effect. In the following months, 15,000 companies and over 500 banks became bankrupt, and the unemployment rate soared. Scholars estimate the rates went as high as 19 percent nationwide, with the hardest-hit states being New York with 35 percent and Michigan with 43 percent.

The effect on the railroad industry was devastating. By 1894, about one-fourth of the entire mileage of the railways was under bankruptcy. Many lost their jobs, while others suffered pay cut after pay cut. This eventually led to a nationwide railroad worker strike in mid-1894. It started with a strike of the Pullman Car Company laborers in Chicago, but it was supported by the American Railway Union, which was one of the largest workers' syndicates of the time. It then spread across the US. The federal government once again intervened with force, stifling out the strike after more than two months.

The so-called Pullman strike of 1894; the illustration shows workers blocking the railroad. Source: https://commons.wikimedia.org

The economic depression lasted until 1897. By this point, both the world and the United States began recovering after years of high unemployment and starvation. Due to the rising economy, railroad companies began to recuperate as well. The pace of building new tracks increased, new workers were employed, and company ownership began consolidating, which was once again led by Morgan, among others. By 1900, seven companies controlled about two-thirds of the nation's railroads. By then, it was a multimillion-dollar business, as the railroads covered more than 193,000 miles (311,000 kilometers).

Despite all the ups and downs of the railroad industry, it proved to be an irreplaceable cog in the economic development of the US, just as it was in other industrializing nations of the time like France, Germany, and Britain. On a more obvious level, railways connected the nation, easing the transportation of raw materials, finished goods, and people and creating a unified market in the United States. It made the flow of money easier and gave an important boost to the economy.

In a similar fashion, the railroads themselves proved to be a major consumer of various raw materials like steel, wood, and coal, as well as numerous finished goods like train cars. This fueled other industrial branches, creating a ripple effect in the economy. As railway companies expanded, other industries had to follow if the expansion was to be continued. Unlike those other businesses, railroad companies were much larger ventures, with subdivisions, workers, and equipment far away from the direct control of the headquarters. Furthermore, operating a railway network safely and efficiently needed a much higher level of organization and cooperation across substantially vaster geographical areas.

This prompted developments of large-scale management bureaucracy in the railroad industry. Later on, those innovations helped other industrial branches to expand from a single factory into large corporations with numerous departments. Since they were such extensive enterprises, the railroad companies employed a large number of workers, both skilled and unskilled, as well as the new managerial class. This also helped to fuel the expanding US economy.

Nonetheless, the railroads had their negative traits as well. The thirst for profit caused many companies to build too many tracks, often where they were not necessary, while others were managed poorly. The working conditions, railway constructions, and maintenance were often criminal, leading to numerous accidents. If that wasn't enough, the high revenue attracted shady businessmen and politicians. The railroad magnates practically invented lobbying, which came to the point of outright bribery of government officials in an attempt to acquire land, rights, or other necessary political or bureaucratic backings from the state, even when it was at the expense of the common population.

Regardless of that dark underbelly, the railroad industry reshaped the society of the United States. Train stations often became the social centers of towns, with an array of other businesses, like hotels and bars, popping up around it. In some cases, whole towns were founded just because the railroad went through there. Railroads also eased the westward expansion of the United States, connecting the frontier to the urban centers. Because of that, railroads became a part of the classic Wild West iconography.

If all of that wasn't enough, trains remained the main mode of transportation in the United States until the mid-20th century, cementing their place in American history.

"Black Gold Fever": The Oil Business Starts

If there is one industry that can accurately encompass that omnipresent feeling during the Gilded Age of outlandish business deals, it would be the oil business. Authors Michael Economides and Ronald Oligney could not have said it better in their book, *The Color of Oil: The History, the Money and the Politics of the World's Biggest Business*:

> No industry better exemplifies certain traits that define the American character: the "can do" attitude practiced under particularly hostile conditions; the piecing together of apparently irreconcilable geographic, political, financial, and technical elements; and the frequent overexploitation of relationships and opportunities with abandon—a kind of *forced serendipity.* The industry's toughness is often credited to the ruthless and enduring boom-and-bust cycles.

What became the main game-changer in terms of energy, geopolitics, and vast economic power during the 20th and 21st centuries began as a humble enterprise. It was developed in 1859 by Colonel Edwin Drake in Titusville, Pennsylvania. This visionary man, who died practically penniless despite being considered the pioneer of one of the world's largest businesses, developed a series of techniques that enabled a far more effective way to drill oil wells.

During those times, oil was basically a waste product. There were no gasoline-chugging vehicles back then. Yet from the mid-1850s on, its efficiency as a source of energy was adapted to a crucial aspect of everyone's lives: lighting. Everything would radically change from then on. Petroleum-derived kerosene lamps started substituting their less-effective predecessors, which used whale oil and coal. This alone sparked a wild race to find petroleum in America and eventually throughout the whole world.

Barely a few months after Colonel Drake's successful drilling of his well, hundreds of other entrepreneurs had adapted his methods. Sadly for Drake, he never got to patent his inventions. Thousands of new barrels flooded the market, making oil prices go from 15 dollars per barrel to barely 10 cents a couple of years later. Many tycoons, who thought they had struck gold by heavily investing in this fledgling business, went bust. Yet Americans ended up receiving the greatest benefits. What had been the privilege of a few prosperous, large cities, as they had the ability to light part of their streets with kerosene lamp posts, or of wealthy homes, which were able to afford the cost of such a luxury, became an inexpensive commodity for practically every household, every urban settlement, and every business.

By the late 19th century, kerosene lamps were commonplace in hospitals, factories, theaters, hospitals, streets, ships, and lighthouses, among many other places. Kerosene stoves and heaters were also developed. This marvelous new way to light people's lives allowed for a more modern lifestyle. Cities became bright, with the possibility of never-before-seen 24-hour activity. And there had not been a better way for winters to become less chilly than with kerosene, at least until electricity came to substitute it with even greater efficiency. Gas lighting already existed, but it was mostly limited to urban areas; it also had the downside of potential explosions and was more expensive. Kerosene lamps were portable, cheap, far less contaminating than their coal counterparts, and less smelly than those using tallow or whale oil.

And kerosene was not the only product made out of oil. A whole new range of other goods also came to the market, such as lubricants for machine parts, paraffin for food preservation, and petroleum jelly. All of this happened years before the invention of the internal-combustion car, which would use gasoline, the oil-derived cash winner of all times.

One man stands out in the way he seized the opportunity to capitalize on this new industry. His business savvy—as well as ruthless methods—would eventually make him become the richest man on Earth, even after the forced breakup of his first company. This man was John D. Rockefeller, the founder of Standard Oil.

Rockefeller, a quiet young man originally from New York State, came into the picture a few years after Colonel Drake made his debut. Rockefeller's family had relocated to Cleveland, Ohio, one of those recently founded Midwestern urban settlements, which profited from the different commerce opportunities of the final Civil War years, as well as from the booming oil business. This go-getter atmosphere would eventually set this city as one of the foremost places to experience America's industrial expansion.

By 1865, twenty-six-year-old Rockefeller was already the part-owner of a successful oil refinery. Yet his partner wanted out; he thought the oil business had too many ups and downs for his conservative views. Rockefeller bought his shares through an auction, where the bidding started at $500. The shares reached $72,500 in the end, which equates to roughly about $1 million today. After this transaction, Rockefeller, who was seen by many as inward and even ascetic, would never stop becoming richer and richer. He acquired, by some estimates, the largest fortune of all time. At the time of his death in 1937, his net worth was around $1.4 billion. Adjusted for inflation, Rockefeller's wealth would be roughly $350 billion today, and it was one that was self-made, not by being an heir or a prince.

The vast wealth Rockefeller amassed came with a catch. In order to achieve this kind of success, he had to be completely merciless with his competitors, cunning in his methods, and highly organized and methodical. The disorganized oil business was transformed by this tycoon—the stereotypical "robber baron"—into a highly centralized corporate business. The timing was perfect; the unstable years of the Civil War were over, and by 1865, America was set for large-scale economic growth. And the demand for ever-increasing amounts of kerosene for home, work, and entertainment provided for such an opportunity.

A caricature depicting Standard Oil monopoly as an octopus controlling the nation. Source: https://commons.wikimedia.org

In his famous Pulitzer-Prize-winner book on oil, *The Prize*, Daniel Yergin stresses that this era in the United States was one of "rapid development, of fiery speculation, and fierce competition...Large-scale enterprises rose in conjunction with technological advances in industries as diverse as steel, meat packing, and communication. Heavy immigration and the opening of the West made for rapidly growing markets." This energetic atmosphere in US business was what Rockefeller called "the Great Game."

Barely a few years later, Standard Oil dominated approximately 90 percent of America's oil refining business—in other words, it was a true monopoly. The company strived to offer products of great quality, incorporating new technologies to become more productive and allow lower prices. However, Rockefeller didn't stop at oil production and refining technology. He strived to eliminate all possible middlemen, products, and services of other companies. Thus, Standard Oil slowly began producing barrels and other equipment. It took control of oil pipelines, storage facilities, and even railroad tank cars. The company also kept large amounts of cash reserves to make it independent of banks in case of a crisis, making it incredibly independent.

To achieve such an overwhelming presence, Rockefeller began buying out his competition, forcing those who refused to sell into bankruptcy. He was merciless in his quest for money and power. Yergin reflects that Rockefeller was "admired by some as a genius of management and organization, he also came to rank as the most hated and reviled American businessman—in part because he was so ruthless and in part because he was so successful."

Rockefeller's company was denounced as "autocratic," and it was common to hear scathing remarks regarding that "gang of thieves." Nonetheless, there was no lack of capability in Rockefeller's inner circle. He and his advisors realized they needed a more efficient control of their business interests. To achieve that, they organized all of his companies into the Standard Oil Trust in 1882. It was a novel business organization, in which stockholders in various Standard Oil enterprises conveyed their stock to nine trustees, giving them full control over all Standard Oil businesses in return for annual dividends.

Due to exposés in the press and courts, public opinion eventually set the tide against Standard Oil and its handful of shareholders, which included Rockefeller's brother, William. This giant corporation would eventually become the centerpiece example for the already-mentioned Sherman Antitrust Act of 1890. This novel legal measure did not signal the end of uber-rich tycoons, but most of them were compelled to break up their monopolies and adapt regulated business standards with fairer commercial and industrial practices.

As a result, Ohio's Supreme Court ordered the Standard Oil Trust to be dissolved in 1892. However, Rockefeller gradually perfected the idea of the holding company; in other words, a company that controlled other companies by holding all or at least a majority of their stock. Over the next two decades, he and Standard Oil adapted to the ever-changing legal landscape of the US economy until it was finally broken up into thirty-four different companies in 1913. Among them were forerunners of corporations like Chevron, Exxon, and Mobil, with the latter two merging back together.

Laying the Foundation: The Age of Steel

Since the beginning of the Industrial Revolution in 18th-century Britain, the iron industry played an important role in the economy. It provided much-needed materials for various machines and tools. It was the same for the United States. By the late 1860s, the iron industry accounted for more than 6 percent of employed workers, as well as almost 8 percent of total manufacturing output. However, iron had numerous shortcomings as a material, mainly in its strength and fracture resistance. The solution for that was steel, which is an iron alloy with added carbon. Steel is more durable and even applicable in construction works.

However, unlike iron, steel was expensive, as it could only be made from wrought iron and in small quantities. This changed in 1855 when a British inventor, Sir Henry Bessemer, developed a process in which steel could be produced quickly, easily, and directly from crude iron. This would revolutionize the iron industry, basically transforming it into the steel industry.

Among the first in the world to realize that was Andrew Carnegie, a self-made businessman who immigrated from Scotland to the US as a teenager. In his youth, he worked up the ladder in the Pennsylvania Railroad Company, learning not only managerial skills but also about the related economy branches, like the iron industry and bridgebuilding. Along the way, Carnegie secured business connections and starting capital.

After the Civil War, Carnegie decided to step away from the railroads, focusing his capital and knowledge on ironworks. He had some investments in that industry prior to the war, but after the war ended, he acquired and opened new mills. He soon began producing rails, selling them to his railroad connections. To expand his business, he also opened the Keystone Bridge Company, which erected iron bridges.

By the early 1870s, Carnegie was introduced to the Bessemer process, which hadn't yet been implemented in the US. As he was a keen businessman, he realized the potential of this technological advancement, and by 1875, his first Bessemer steel mill was opened. Carnegie was now able to sell steel cheaper and make it in larger quantities. At that moment, a steel magnate was formed.

Carnegie went on to expand his steel business, continuously searching for other technical innovations to reduce operating costs. He also used the economic depressions to his advantage by buying out his struggling competitors, forming somewhat a monopoly of his own. Furthermore, Carnegie had similar ideas as Rockefeller, as he bought businesses that supported his steelworks. Thus, he owned coal fields, coke furnaces, iron fields, local railways, and steamboat lines. By 1892, he merged all of his assets into Carnegie Steel.

The result of his effort was shown in the rise of steel production in the US, which went from about 150,000 tons in the early 1870s to 1.4 million tons in 1880. At the same time, he cut the cost from $100 per ton to about $50 in the late 1870s, all the way down to $18 in 1890. Along the way, Carnegie became immensely rich.

Though he wasn't as hated or remembered as being as vile as many other robber barons, Carnegie was quite ferocious and aggressive. He was ready to abuse his influence, and some claim he even became a compulsive liar. The steel magnate was also radically opposed to the idea of unionized labor, and he used private security to violently quell the Homestead steel strike of 1892. This event proved to be a major setback in the unionization of steelworkers.

By 1900, Carnegie's steel empire was working like a Swiss clock, despite feeling the repercussions of the 1890s economic depression when the demand for steel fell noticeably. Despite the crisis, by the beginning of the 20th century, the US produced about ten million tons of steel, becoming a leading producer in the world above both Britain and Germany. However, by then, Carnegie, who was in his late sixties, had decided to retire.

In 1901, he sold Carnegie Steel Company to no other than J. P. Morgan. At the time, Morgan and one of Carnegie's employees realized that the solution for the steel industry was consolidation. Besides Carnegie's company, Morgan also acquired several other major steel producers to form US Steel. Its capital was deemed at around 1.5 billion dollars, becoming the first billion-dollar corporation in history. In the year of its formation, US Steel had over 200 manufacturing mills, 41 mines, and about a thousand miles of railroad. It accounted for about two-thirds of America's entire steel output, just shy of 30 percent of the world's production.

It was clear that steel was a crucial component of the economy, a true material for the future.

Kindhearted Bandits

The Gilded Age was a time of numerous contradictions. It was a period of economic growth, yet it included two major economic crises. Companies rose and fell, and men became wealthy before going broke. Workers were being exploited and violently suppressed, yet they lived better than in previous times in history. On top of the economic food chain were the already-mentioned robber barons. These men were ferocious and borderline criminal, and they were feared as much as they were respected.

Yet looking deeper at some personal examples of the robber barons, we can find the contradictions so entwined into the Gilded Age. Despite grabbing for power and wealth, a number of the robber barons eventually became famous for their philanthropic actions. Large portions of their fortunes went toward educational, cultural, and social causes, with their names remaining in some of the most iconic buildings and theaters across America.

Carnegie's philanthropy in a caricature.
Source: https://commons.wikimedia.org

Most notable in these philanthropic areas were Rockefeller and Carnegie. Regardless of their ruthlessness in business, they felt it was their duty to give back to the community.

Rockefeller believed his wealth was a public trust awarded by God, so he began donating to numerous educational institutions, primarily in the field of medicine. His foundations also supported programs for schooling the African American population in the South. All of that generosity was part of Rockefeller's Baptist beliefs. By the time he died in 1937, Rockefeller had donated more than $500 million, which surpasses $100 billion when converted to the modern dollar.

Carnegie had similar ideals, as he dispensed his wealth to erect thousands of libraries, parks, hospitals, meeting and concert halls, and churches while also donating to universities and education as well. Overall, he donated around $350 million to charitable activities, some $75 billion by today's standards. At one point in his life, Carnegie even noted that amassing wealth was one of the worst types of idolatry, as the worship of money is one of the most degrading. Thus, Carnegie is the perfect example of the contradictions present during the Gilded Age.

Chapter 4 – Ups and Downs of Politics and the Government

The latter half of the 19th century proved to be a rather turbulent time in the United States. After going through the terrors of war, which caused incredible damage both in the realms of material goods as well to national unity, the US was on a historical seesaw. It could have gone either way from that point, and it seems it went both up and down.

The Nature of Politics

The changes in the social landscape of the healing nation were quickly reflected in its politics. During this time, the US grew both in population and in sheer size. The westward expansion continued, powered by the growing industries, agriculture, railroads, and immigration. New states were formed from the unorganized territories. To clarify, those lands were *de jure* part of the United States, but they weren't fully politically connected and incorporated into the system. After the Civil War, the number of states grew, which included the admission of Nebraska (1867); Colorado (1876); North Dakota, South Dakota, Montana, and Washington (1889); Idaho and Wyoming (1890); and finally, Utah (1896).

This meant that the governmental apparatus grew, both in federal and local terms. This can be represented by simple numbers. In 1871, it was estimated that the US federal government employed about 51,000 people. By 1901, that number had passed 250,000 while continuing to grow. It is interesting to point out that a large number of those employed by the federal government served as postal workers. Just about 6,000 of the employees in 1871 worked in Washington, DC.

Despite the growth of the federal government, the Gilded Age remained mostly influenced by local and state politics. This was because federal politics had a much less pronounced influence on the everyday lives of common Americans. It was the local and, to an extent, state governments that helped the people find jobs, feed their families, build infrastructure, etc. The reach of the federal government was far from that level of impact on people's lives.

The expansion in population and the growing industries also brought the rise of urban life in the US, which prompted another shift in politics. Politicians' power in the urban centers, where the masses were gathered into a small area, grew immensely. This was only heightened by the remarkable level of organization they had. On top was a single "political boss," who was surrounded by a number of committee members and district captains. The boss gave orders and "ruled" as he saw fit, while his subordinates helped. Below them were organized voters, who were separated into precincts and districts.

This local political organization provided common Americans with jobs and charitable donations in the form of money or food. They were also the ones who built and organized citywide services, like transportation, lighting, and education, while also building housing, parks, paved roads, etc. However, these improvements were usually of secondary concern, as their primary goal was to gather voters. Thus, these urban service upgrades were usually only built if the politicians could sway neighborhood constituents.

Besides those large promotions, city bosses also planned parades, free banquets, and firework displays, all with the help of their loyal voters.

Another common form of political power struggles on a local level was through the buying and selling of votes and taking bribes. Thus, local politics proved to be quite a fertile ground for corruption, especially when wealthy businessmen with deep pockets needed something to improve their business or break up a strike.

Similar political practices occurred on the larger political scale as well. Party officials were organized from the top of the federal level all the way down to the local branches. The local party members took care of their constituents by providing jobs and distributing food or fuel, while the business supporters were kept loyal by mechanisms of patronage and favoritism. The loyalty of local party members was ensured by the distribution of public offices, which were also used for the recruitment of new members.

Looking at federal politics, one will notice that the nature remained the same but that the scale grew. Better paid federal jobs were offered, larger political gatherings were organized, and even the briberies were amplified. For example, securing land grants for hundreds of acres would net politicians tens of thousands of dollars, if not hundreds.

On that nationwide political stage, like throughout most of US history, only two parties played in these major roles. Of course, it was the Democratic and the Republican Parties. Both of those parties avoided dealing with controversial problems or adventurous initiatives, as they were too risky and the political gain minimal. Furthermore, both parties were closely tied, making it quite hard to achieve any major political changes during the late 19th century.

That kind of political stalemate was also expressed in the government. Throughout the Gilded Age, the Democrats usually controlled the House of Representatives while the Republicans controlled the Senate. The same party holding the presidency and the Congress majority was a seldom occurrence, happening only during a few years of the Gilded Age.

The White House lost much of its influence during this period. Congress was seen as the main body in which national policies were formed. This view was embodied by a statement from an Ohio senator, who said that the president should only obey and enforce the law. This can be partially explained by the fact that no president won the popular vote from 1872 to 1896. Thus, from Lincoln to Theodore Roosevelt, there were no strong, remarkable, or memorable presidents. Despite that, it is important to note that during the Gilded Age, thanks to wider support in a number of states, the Republicans won most of the presidential elections.

The feeling of a political stalemate was only heightened by the fact that both parties differed little when it came to significant issues, like regulation of big business, civil reforms, currency, and immigration. This was occasionally disrupted by third parties, like, for example, the Populists or Prohibitionists. However, the reach of the third parties was limited, as they focused and appealed to particular questions, such as inflation or temperance legislation.

It would be somewhat expected that the deadlock of national politics and the grittiness of local politics would lead to indifference and the low turnout of voters. However, it was quite the opposite. During the Gilded Age, about 70 to 80 percent of the people exercised their voting rights. These high numbers could be explained by several factors.

One is that for hundreds of thousands of citizens, the election results provided an answer on whether they could keep their government jobs. Other grander ideas and policies were of lesser concern for many of them.

Another part of the explanation was that politics at the time was somewhat of an entertainment for the masses. Faithful voters were often quite enthusiastic, taking part in rallies and picnics and gulping down newspaper articles regarding politics. A sense of camaraderie developed between party members. In that sense, it could be compared to the sports fans of today, as this party allegiance was passed on through the generations.

Religion and moral norms also played a role. The Republican Party tended to gather around Protestants, and they usually held conservative moralist beliefs. Many of them felt it was their duty to vote. In contrast, the Democrats gathered a coalition of various smaller religious groups in the US, such as Catholics and Jews, as well as those with fewer concerns about religion. They felt they needed to oppose the moral oppression that restricted their way of life.

Finally, to certain members of society, choosing a like-minded candidate meant a difference between being an equal citizen or an oppressed outcast. This was especially true for African Americans in the South and immigrants, whose rights remained uncertain at the time.

The US at Home: Gilded Age Domestic Policies

For the most part, the domestic policy of the early Gilded Age was focused on remedying the consequences of the Civil War. These policies belonged more to the Reconstruction era, though it fell into the early 1870s. Nonetheless, that story has already been told in a previous chapter, so we will begin with 1877. By this point, the Gilded Age had been around for seven years already.

That year, Republican candidate Rutherford B. Hayes became president, and the Reconstruction Era had officially ended with the withdrawal of the Union troops from the South. Soon after assuming office, Hayes was faced with the Great Railroad Strike of 1877. Hayes's answer was to send federal troops to take care of the rioting laborers, which is quite a conservative approach. This was his stance when it came to the economy as well, as he vetoed the 1878 Bland-Allison Act, which aimed to minimally increase the supply of silver coins. Despite that, US Congress, which had a Republican majority, overruled his veto, restoring the silver standard of the dollar along with the golden one.

However, that wasn't the only disagreement that Hayes had with his own party. Over the course of his presidency, he fought hard against the spoils system, acknowledging public discontent over the matter of corruption. It was Hayes who first introduced the merit system, which was, by then, long established in the European industrial nations, such as France, Britain, and Germany. Disregarding the discontent of other Republican leaders, Rutherford B. Hayes began employing citizens based on their capabilities and qualifications, disregarding political affiliation. Additionally, he pledged that no government employee would be forced to give political contributions. On top of that, Hayes banned civil servants from participating in election campaigns, though he didn't infringe on their voting rights.

Photograph of Hayes's inauguration.
Source: https://commons.wikimedia.org

Both Hayes and the Republican Party were disappointed with each other, prompting a new Republican candidate for the presidential election of 1880. This time, the party chose James Garfield. He seemed like he was cut out to be a good president. He won the elections, despite not winning the popular vote, and he assumed office in early 1881. However, he was never given an opportunity to prove his worth, for he was assassinated in July of that year by a disgruntled office seeker. Intriguingly enough, his murderer was also a Republican, though he was from a radical faction within the party.

Chester A. Arthur, Garfield's vice president, took over the office. The circumstances of his rise to the presidency allowed him to distance himself from the more radical wing of the Republican Party, which advocated the spoils system and more traditional politics. Furthermore, the Republicans had lost their majority in Congress. These facts allowed Arthur to change his political stance, and he started advocating for civil reforms. By early 1883, together with an overwhelming majority in Congress, the Pendleton Civil Service Reform Act was passed. The Federal Civil Service Commission was also reestablished, which regulated employment in the federal sector. Merit came above partisanship, and competitive examination became the basis for the growing number of governmental jobs.

Arthur also exhibited a more liberal economic stance, as he advocated the lowering of income taxes. High tariffs were imposed in the Civil War era to discourage foreign imports and safeguard US manufacturers. However, by the early 1880s, the amount of money that was sitting in the Treasury began to lower circulation and slow down economic growth. Arthur wanted to lower the taxes, but he faced strong opposition. The result was mixed, as the so-called "mongrel tariff" of 1883 only lowered taxes on some commodities, showcasing the power of interest groups in Congress.

The next president was a Democratic candidate named Grover Cleveland, who won the 1884 election mostly due to the blunders of the Republican campaign. Cleveland was a reformist of high ideals. On the one hand, he believed in a minimalistic role of the government, which was starkly expressed when he refused to aid Texan farmers as droughts plagued them in 1887. He felt the government should only interfere when the issue was directly tied to the public service or benefit. Otherwise, the government would become too paternalistic and the citizens too dependent.

Despite that, Cleveland pushed for some major reforms. One was related to the railroads, as he sought to regulate interstate lines. In 1887, he signed an act, creating the Interstate Commerce Commission (ICC), which clashed with big business. However, the reach of this commission was quite limited, as the law's wording was too vague and weak. In a further challenge to big business, Cleveland pushed for lower tariffs. He and critics of high import taxes argued that they allowed large corporations to foster an ironclad grip over the US market by preventing imports and impeding smaller manufacturers. However, Cleveland lost this fight, as the Republicans blocked it in Congress.

Nonetheless, the tariff issue became a central debate point in the 1888 election. This time, though, the Republicans won, thanks to no less than $3 million, which was either donated by their supporters in big business or came from some shady campaign tactics. Although Cleveland won the popular vote, Benjamin Harrison was the one who took over the presidency, as he had won the electoral vote.

In the first two years of his presidency, Harrison was supported by the Republican majority in Congress. This allowed him to pass several important laws. One of the more important ones was the Sherman Antitrust Act of 1890, which aimed to curb big business monopolies. However, it turned out to be a largely symbolic victory, as, by 1901, it had only been acted upon eighteen times. Besides that, Harrison passed a law that awarded Civil War veterans with pensions. More controversial was the McKinley Tariff Act. Due to this act, import taxes were raised higher than ever before. This resulted in a major public backlash, as big corporations had even less competition, and prices slowly began to rise.

Still, the most crucial problem that the Harrison Cabinet faced was the shrinking of money in circulation. This was largely caused by years of emphasis on the gold-backed dollar, despite the official bimetallism of the US currency. Harrison tried to rectify this with the Sherman Silver Purchase Act of 1890, which directed that the Treasury had to buy silver on a monthly basis, reducing the nation's dependency on gold. Nonetheless, the measure proved to be largely inadequate. The worldwide deflation of gold was slowly leading to the reduction of income, while the debts of many citizens remained the same.

If that wasn't enough, Harrison also faced a farming problem, as years of uncontrolled economic practices had led to an agriculture crisis. Throughout the years, US agrarian output grew because of the expansion of farmable land and the development of agrarian technology and know-how. This led to overproduction, which led to falling prices of important food crops, like wheat and corn. Even cotton prices fell, which was an important crop in the still largely unindustrialized South.

Along with their progressively lower incomes, farmers also faced rising prices in railroad transports. Furthermore, high income taxes allowed big corporations to raise the prices of manufactured goods farmers needed to work the lands. Finally, most of their products were sold in foreign markets, where rising international competition diminished the prices. And at the same time, their debts continued to rise, meaning they entered a vicious cycle. To raise more crops, farmers needed loans, and to repay those loans, they needed more crops. All of this led to the further dropping of prices. By 1890, the farmers had had enough, and they began to voice their resentment with the entire system.

Prior organizations and alliances had proven unable to fight for farmers' needs. This time, farmers across several states began to organize into parties. This eventually culminated in the forming of the Populist Party (also known as the People's Party). The focus of this new party was on inflation, antitrust laws, railroad regulations, the functionality of the US Department of Agriculture, and more available farm-based credits. The Populists had some local success, as they won seats in several state legislatures, as well as a single senator from Kansas. This prompted the Populists to try their luck in the 1892 presidential elections.

Their ideas and policies resonated with many, but their candidate lacked charisma and enthusiasm. Additionally, their relatively young party was unable to oppose the organizational capabilities of the other two major parties or match their big business funded campaigns. Nonetheless, the Populists managed to gather about one million voters and twenty-two electoral votes, a rare example of a third party leaving a mark on the presidential election. Both the Republicans and the Democrats chose the same candidates as in 1888, which meant Benjamin Harris and Grover Cleveland faced off once again. It was a close race, but Grover managed to edge ahead in both the popular and electoral votes. This could be partially explained by the fact that the Populists took some of the traditionally Republican voters and states. Another reason was the failure of many Republican policies. That would explain why Cleveland had 400,000 more popular votes, which was the largest margin since the beginning of the Gilded Age.

Just days before Grover Cleveland took over for his second term in office, the Panic of 1893 struck. As previously mentioned, it began with the fall of a single railroad company before quickly spreading across the nation, hitting all branches of the economy. Thousands of businesses closed, and one-fourth of all unskilled laborers lost their jobs. On top of that, by 1894, more than 10,000 farm mortgages were foreclosed in Kansas alone. Farmers across the nation lost ownership of their land; by 1900, around one-third of them were mere tenants.

Cleveland, in accordance with his ideas of a minimalistic government, did little to ease the immediate troubles of the population, though soup kitchens were opened to ease the famine. Instead, he went the conservative way, repealing the Sherman Silver Purchase Act, which returned the dollar to the gold standard. This only constricted the amount of circulating money, and that effect was furthered when investors started exchanging their silver for gold. Cleveland took a positive step with a tariff act that lowered income taxes. However, after the bill passed, big business lobbied Congress, and hundreds of amendments minimalized its effect. Even the president himself called the act shameful, despite advocating it from the start.

Then, in 1894, the Pullman strike blocked the functionality of the nation. Besides slowing down commerce and communication, the railway blockade impeded the post office. Furthermore, a sizeable chunk of affected lines was under the control of the federal government through a receivership. This was enough cause for Cleveland to feel federal action was warranted. In a display of his sternness, he sent federal troops to break up the strike without giving the workers a chance to negotiate. The action was heralded by representatives of both major parties, yet the public was shocked and revolted.

National Guard protecting a factory during the Pullman strike.
Source: https://commons.wikimedia.org

Due to this political climate, the Democrats were crushed in the 1894 mid-term election. The majority of the seats went to the Republicans, but even the Populists saw a rise in their representation. Two years later, the economy was slowly reviving, yet the effects of the economic depression were still felt. As the parties approached the presidential elections of 1896, the main political topic was still the coinage issue.

The Democratic Party saw an internal shift, which was partially caused by their overall loss of support. They turned to William Jennings Bryan, who advocated for liberal reforms, federal welfare, and taxation of the rich; he also stood on the pro-silver side. The Populist Party supported him, as they feared a two-way split between the Populists and Democrats, who shared similar ideals, would only lead to the demise of their political agenda. Due to this, the Populist Party lost its identity and ceased to exist as a political faction.

Opposing Bryan was William McKinley. McKinley was a conservative politician who stood for the ideals of the Gilded Age; he was pro-gold, believed in higher taxes and restoring industrial production, and was in favor of big business. As such, his campaign received substantial support from business magnates, and thanks to their deeper pockets, his campaign was better organized. Over 1,400 Republican speakers traveled across the US, spreading his message. In the end, this was enough for him to win the election, despite Bryan having more charisma. It is worth noting that McKinley's victory was likely helped by the fact that some of the Democrats, who supported more conservative Cleveland politics, were agitated by Bryan enough to publicly state it wasn't a shame if their voters supported McKinley.

Regardless of the results, the 1896 presidential election was crucial. It marked the transition into a new form of campaigning, which was more professional and wider-reaching. Also, the fact that two million more voters turned out than in the election of 1892 exhibits how serious an election this was to most Americans.

By the time McKinley had sworn into office in early 1897, the economic crisis was largely alleviated. The industry was getting back on its feet. The Republican president sought to support this by raising the import taxes, though he left a reciprocity clause in the act. This allowed for mutual tax reduction in trade between the nations. His office later reached such agreements with foreign governments, but the US Senate never ratified them.

Furthermore, adhering to his campaign, McKinley doubled down on the gold-backed dollar, signing the Gold Standard Act in 1900. The shortage of gold had been lessened worldwide due to the gold rushes in Canada and Australia, which made pro-silver policies lose support outside of its base. Furthermore, McKinley's presidency showed a lax attitude toward trusts and corporations, as McKinley saw the economic benefits of the consolidation of big business. Unlike his other beliefs, this one proved less popular among the public; however, at the time, it still wasn't a burning issue.

Due to his great popularity, McKinley ran for a second term in 1900. He was once again pitted against Bryan. However, due to the success of his previous term, McKinley easily won, winning almost 900,000 more popular votes. Unfortunately, his second tenure in the White House was cut short in September 1901 when he was assassinated. His vice president, Theodore Roosevelt, a rising star among the Republicans, took over, marking a new era in US politics.

The Gilded Age politics was marked by the dominance of the Republican Party. Only Grover Cleveland was able to break their winning streak, though he managed to do so twice. Even so, his politics weren't too divergent from other Republican presidents, as they were, for the most part, in favor of developing big business and industrialization. Interestingly enough, the Gilded Age was also marked by the political dominance of Ohio, as five out of seven presidents hailed from that state, with the exceptions being Cleveland and Chester Arthur.

As the US entered a new century, the two leading parties found themselves in somewhat switched roles. Overall, the Republicans became a more stern and conservative party, one that was in favor of corporate capitalism, while the Democrats turned toward taking a more liberal stance, one that was in favor of reforms and more substantial federal aid. This basic division of the political ideologies between the two parties is still present in the political landscape of the modern-day United States.

Rising Imperialism: US Foreign Policy of Gilded Age

As with many aspects of American society, economy, and politics, foreign policy changed considerably during the Gilded Age. Up until the Civil War, the primary focus of the US was its expansion westward, which was expressed in the ideals of Manifest Destiny. At the same time, Washington sought to limit the influence of European empires on the American continent, which was embodied in the Monroe Doctrine.

Due to the chaos caused by the war, the US lowered its focus on foreign policies. Yet the tentative support of the British toward the Confederacy raised many eyebrows in the Union. Although it was not involved enough to spark a full-blown conflict between the two nations, the relations between the US and Britain worsened. Simultaneously, France expanded its foothold on the continent by making Mexico its puppet state in 1862. By the end of the Civil War, two European powers surrounded the US through their positions in Canada and Mexico.

Tensions were high, and the US posted strong forces on its borders with Mexico while simultaneously allowing Mexican rebels to get supplies on their territory. The pressure was high enough for France to retreat from Mexico; by 1867, the puppet regime was overthrown. Soon afterward, the regime changed in France as a result of a failed war with Germany in 1870. As the short-lived monarchical power was substituted with a new republican government, US-French relations quickly improved. This was symbolized by the Statue of Liberty, which France sent to the United States in 1884. Despite that, trade remained limited due to high taxes, while an insignificant number of French people migrated to the US. The good relations continued throughout the Gilded Age and into the 20th century.

Relations with Britain proved rockier than that. Due to their unofficial support of the Confederacy, many Americans saw the British as their chief opponents once again. The public demanded retribution, either in huge sums of money or in the British territories in Canada. The latter option fit snugly both in the Monroe Doctrine and Manifest Destiny. Of course, Britain wouldn't simply roll over and meet the demands of its former colony.

As one can expect, tensions were high, and they were only worsened by the so-called Fenian raids of 1866 and 1870. The Fenian Brotherhood was an organization of the Irish population in the US, and they sought to support Irish independence through its pressure on British Canada. The US government looked the other way when this organization intruded on Canadian soil, attacking British soldiers stationed there.

The relations between the two countries saw a slow rise in the 1870s. This was helped by the fact that the Fenians disbanded on their own, and the British Empire also agreed to pay $15.5 million of retributions for their Civil War entanglements in 1872, though only after international arbitrage. From then on, relations recovered, though both sides remained somewhat untrustworthy of each other, as their interests often collided.

In 1867, Canada achieved its independence, becoming a British dominion. This meant that Canadians controlled internal affairs, while diplomacy and defense policy was under British regulation. During the course of the 19th century, Britain slowly relinquished its tight grip over Canada, helping both their relations with the US and the relations between the US and Canada.

While these relationships were a clear continuation of previous foreign policies, including the protectionist tariffs, new ideas began crystalizing after the Civil War. By the late 1860s, the US already stretched across the width of the North American continent, even though a considerable chunk of its territories weren't yet colonized and fully incorporated into the nation. Some American politicians began looking outward.

The first step toward this was made by William Seward, who was the secretary of state under Andrew Johnson. He realized that the US would one day need to expand into the Pacific, primarily to achieve economic dominance over the East Asian markets. To accomplish that, he wanted to acquire Alaska from the Russian Empire in 1867 for a measly $7.2 million. Despite being seen as an empty icebox, it was a strategic move. It furthered the US foothold into the Pacific while simultaneously blocking any further advances of the British in Canada.

Seward also hoped this move would prompt British Columbia to join the US or that Britain would offer this territory instead of monetary compensation for their transgressions during the Civil War. Of course, this never came to fruition.

Presidents Johnson (up) and Grant (down).
Source: *https://commons.wikimedia.org*

Two years later, Grant's administration attempted to do something similar with "Santo Domingo" (the modern-day Dominican Republic). There, instability caused by their civil war led to the rise of piracy. This prompted Grant to send the US Navy to deal with them. Through clandestine negotiations, Grant offered to buy Santo Domingo with a hinted possibility of statehood. Grant's justification was woven with the Monroe Doctrine, as he claimed he wanted to do so to protect Santo Domingo from being overtaken by a European nation. Despite that, the Senate refused to ratify the agreement, and this action failed.

Afterward, the focus of the US once again shifted back to the Pacific. In 1871, a small fleet of five ships sailed to Korea, attempting to shift it from its isolationist policy. Something similar was achieved with Japan in 1853; however, their approach failed with the Koreans. After a short skirmish, in which the Americans were victorious, the US threatened further actions. The Koreans ignored this, continuing their isolation for another ten years before opening up to trade with the US in 1881.

Apart from looking at possible markets, the US also scoured for possible footholds in the Pacific. Naturally, the first in line was Hawaii. By the mid-1870s, the Hawaiian Kingdom already had a considerable American population, mostly missionaries and sugar planters. This led to an agreement in 1875, in which Hawaiian sugar became tax-free. In return, the island kingdom promised not to lease or give any parts of its land to third parties. Thus, Hawaii became somewhat of a US dominion.

The United States had more straightforward dealings with the Samoans, as the Hayes's administration signed a treaty with them in 1878. With it, Americans were granted a naval base at Pago Pago, while US citizens were given the right to remain subject only to US law while on Samoan territory. Along with that came trade concessions. The Samoans struck similar agreements with the British and Germans as well.

Arthur's and Cleveland's presidencies remained somewhat silent on the international front. During these times, officials in Washington merely discussed trade deals with South American nations, as well as tried to mediate in a war between Peru, Chile, and Bolivia. Regardless, expansionistic and imperialistic ideals continued to spread throughout the public. Many noted politicians, scholars, and writers began to advocate for a stronger presence of the US on the world stage.

The revival of foreign expansion came with Harrison. His office tried to negotiate a naval base on Haiti, but he failed. On the other side of the world, in 1889, the US managed to secure a shared protectorate over Samoa following a civil war on the islands. It was the first legal protectorate of the US, despite being shared with Germany and Britain. Furthermore, Harrison's office continued the policy of economic expansion in Latin America, signing several reciprocal trade agreements.

In 1891, Hawaii returned as the main topic of foreign affairs. By then, the McKinley Tariff Act had wreaked havoc on the Hawaiian economy, as its sugar lost the favored position on the market. This prompted a reaction from the native population, but the monarchical government was toppled in a coup led by American planters. They then pleaded with Harrison's office to be admitted into the US. However, his presidency ended before he could act on this. Cleveland, who succeeded Harrison, was more reluctant, though. He sent a representative to inspect the situation on the islands. After reading the report, which stated that the majority of Hawaiians were opposed to annexation, Cleveland refused to go through with it. As in his prior term, Grover Cleveland remained opposed to aggressive imperialism.

With the arrival of McKinley in the White House, US foreign policy quickly escalated toward open imperialism. His first goal was to finish the annexation of Hawaii. McKinley used mixed rhetoric to gain support for it. On the one hand, he claimed he wanted to protect the islands from Japan and thus secure US interests in the Pacific. On the other, McKinley placed the Hawaiian issue in the perspective of Manifest Destiny and the supposed right for American expansion. In 1897, McKinley submitted an annexation treaty, which was officially ratified in 1898. Hawaii became a part of the US.

While this agreement was still in Congress, McKinley's office turned toward Cuba and its colonial masters in Spain. An active rebellion against the Spaniards had been going on there since the early 1890s, garnering ever-rising public sympathy in the US. Many were vocal for US intervention, yet no one was louder than future president Theodore Roosevelt. Initially, McKinley was satisfied with a stern warning and giving his overall support to the rebels, but by early 1898, the pressure of public opinion and that of his party comrades proved to be unbearable. After the sinking of the USS *Maine* in Havana Harbor, which was later deemed an accident, McKinley finally declared war in April 1898.

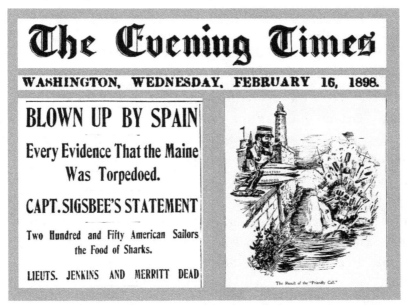

Newspaper cutouts regarding the sinking of the USS Maine.
Source: https://commons.wikimedia.org

The war lasted for just over three months and ended up in a crushing US victory, where the majority of American casualties were caused by diseases. The battles were fought on two fronts: Cuba and the Philippines, which was another part of the Spanish colonial empire. When the war ended, the US took control of Puerto Rico and Guam, which were also former Spanish colonies, as well as the Philippines, while guaranteeing Cuban independence. In return, America paid $20 million to Spain for the infrastructure of the conquered lands.

Despite entering the war with the proclaimed goal of liberating Cuba, the US actually based this venture purely on imperial goals. Cuba was given formal independence, yet it had to cede the harbor of Guantanamo, and its interior and foreign policies remained under the strong supervision of the US. Big business saw a lot of potential on that island. Furthermore, the United States gained two important island harbors, one in the Pacific—Guam—and one in the Caribbean—Puerto Rico. Both became part of the US, yet to this day, they remain unincorporated territories in a political sense. Finally, Americans denied to give independence to the Philippines, calling upon their "civilizatory" mission there, but it was mostly because of its strategic and economic position in Southeast Asia.

By the end of the 19th century, the main drive behind US foreign policy became imperialism, which transformed into Roosevelt's aggressive "big stick diplomacy." The internal opposition to that kind of politics, despite having supporters like Twain and Carnegie, was overwhelmed by the majority of the population. With its victory over Spain, the US stepped onto the stage of great superpowers, and it started acting like that, imposing its worldwide interests by force. This was evident in the events of 1899: the annexation of Samoa, its participation in the division of imperialistic interests in China through the so-called Open Door policy, and the outbreak of a Filipino rebellion, to which the US responded violently. By then, there was no going back to the old ways.

Chapter 5 – Turbulent Winds of Change in the US

The Gilded Age proved to be a period of great change in the United States. Rapid industrialization, increased immigration, internal migration, expansions in the West, urbanization, and many other factors caused societal shifts that had been rarely seen in history. As such, new social groups emerged as more important parts of American society. Some of them were truly new, like certain migrant groups and industrial laborers. Of course, others, like Native Americans, African Americans, and women, had existed since the foundation of the nation, yet they still remained disenfranchised and largely ostracized from society.

However, the rapid transformation of the US allowed some of the existing chains to be at least loosened, if not broken. Yet, like with all other aspects of the Gilded Age, these societal changes weren't always so kind to all. Some groups suffered, while others, despite slight improvements, remained oppressed. In this chapter, we'll try to explore the ups and downs of the overhaul of American society.

Freed but Still Chained: African Americans in the Late 19th Century

After the Civil War, it seemed that the black population in the US was on the fast track to a better future due to their liberation and the constitutional amendments safeguarding their basic rights. However, this quickly proved to be a false hope for many.

With the withdrawal of federal troops in 1877, the African American population in the South lost its official governmental protection. Prior to that, violence and attacks against them occurred, but it was curbed to some degree. Without government soldiers protecting their very existence, the violence against them grew. Mass mobs often attacked and, in some instances, killed African Americans, blaming them for all the bad things that were occurring in their neighborhood. Sometimes local law enforcement would assist, charging African Americans with crimes they didn't commit and sending them to jail or the gallows. The judicial system also failed to protect them, as convictions against African Americans were easily attained.

In cases when the tacit support of local institutions wasn't there or didn't act as quickly as the mob wanted, it was common for them to turn toward lynching. Although this form of illegal capital punishment became somewhat common before the Civil War, it wasn't aimed primarily at blacks. However, with the growing racial tensions, Southern whites began lynching African Americans on a larger scale. Accusations ranged from suspected murder or assault to sleeping with consenting white women (often described as rape) or stealing. For these white men, these charges never needed to go to trial if there was a communal condemnation. So, in many cases, blacks were lynched simply because they were in the wrong place at the wrong time. The main force behind these murders was pure hatred.

*A photograph of three lynched African Americans (up) and a
caricature on black voting rights in the South (down).
Source: https://commons.wikimedia.org*

Another frightening characteristic of lynching was that it was legally murder that took place in public; thus, everyone knows who did it, yet this crime almost always went unpunished. The legal system and law enforcement did nothing to prevent this or penalize the perpetrators. It only exhibited the powerlessness of African Americans. To make matters worse, in some cases, the executions were less humane than a simple hanging. Sometimes the viciousness of the lynching went as far as leaving the victim to slowly starve and suffer for days while tied to a tree. Even worse, there were documented cases of people being slowly burnt alive for hours.

Apart from physical violence, African Americans suffered severely in social and political oppression. During the Reconstruction era, the first segregation laws were passed during the Reconstruction era, a time when American society was supposed to be finding a place for African Americans to enjoy their newfound freedoms. Initially, these laws divided black and white communities by creating separate libraries, schools, transportation, etc. These services were usually underfunded and much worse equipped for the blacks than those intended for the white population. This stopped any possibility for the full societal incorporation of African Americans.

This oppression was only worsened with the already-mentioned Jim Crow laws, which used various tools to limit voting and other rights of the African American population. This kind of political disenfranchisement gained wider traction in the late 1880s and early 1890s, leaving a considerable number of black voters excluded. For example, in 1900, there was just a bit more than 5,000 African Americans on the rolls in Louisiana, despite being a majority in the state.

There were a couple of major reasons why the legislations of Southern states decided to take such a route. One was clearly political, as in many counties, the black population was the majority, allowing them to not only vote for the Republican Party but also to elect their own leaders. As such, they undermined the rule of white Democrats in the South. The white elites were even willing to disenfranchise poor white folks in order to keep their power. The other major reason was, of course, racism and their unhidden disdain toward black people.

However, it would be wrong to limit racism just to Southern whites. Despite opposing slavery as a concept, many Northerners didn't think much of the African American population. Even worse, with the rise of imperialism, the idea of white supremacy, which also permeated European views of the world, began to take hold of parts of America. Whites were simply seen as better and on an ordained mission from God. This helped explain expansion outside of the US, but it also pushed down the black population at home. Furthermore, Northern politicians saw little gain in fighting for the rights of African Americans, as their plight moved away from public concerns. Thus, for most of the Gilded Age, the federal government simply looked the other way when it came to these questions of civil rights.

Even worse, in some cases, the federal government played an active role in diminishing the rights of African Americans, as well as other minorities. An example of that would be the 1883 Supreme Court decision to abolish the Civil Rights Act of 1875. This act legally guaranteed that everyone, regardless of race, was entitled to equal treatment in public accommodations and transportation. The explanation for such a ruling was that it was deemed unconstitutional, as Congress wasn't given the right to control private businesses or persons.

However, once African Americans were given a voice, they were not ready to be silenced once again. A number of prominent civil rights activists, like Booker T. Washington, Ida B. Wells, and W. E. B. Du Bois, continued to speak out publicly about the plight of African Americans while also organizing numerous associations to fight for the cause. Some turned toward the judicial system as a stage for their struggle, like the famous Plessy v. Ferguson case of 1896. Unfortunately, most of those rulings only supported the legality behind the idea of "separate but equal." A number of African Americans used the political arena to carry on their struggle for proper equality; however, the Jim Crow laws made it rather hard for them to reach the higher echelons of government. Thus, there were only eight black congressmen from 1880 to 1900, which was a sharp decline from the fourteen who had served between 1870 and 1880.

It should be mentioned that, at least to some extent, the lives of blacks got better during this period. Some received an education, though not many. Some managed to develop their own careers or businesses, yet most remained farmers, making the 1890s especially tough on them. Probably the most significant thing African Americans gained was the liberty of movement. Throughout the Gilded Age, tens of thousands of African Americans migrated from the South to either the North or the Midwest. Later dubbed "the Great Migration," this was a physical attempt to escape the bigotry, racism, and violence of the South. In their new homes, many blacks became workers in urban centers, trying to find jobs in industry. However, it proved that blacks weren't much more welcome there, as many lower-class Northerners saw them as a threat to their jobs. But at least their lives were relatively safer from the violence and lynchings of the South.

Due to this uphill struggle and almost unchecked violence against African Americans, many scholars consider this part of history as the worst when it came to the lives of blacks in the US, especially at the turn of the century. Though this idea is debatable, as the conditions under slavery were incredibly severe, it indicates just how bad their position and lives were during this era. Therefore, the Gilded Age, which started with a promise of equality for African Americans, only marked the beginning of their cause, which would last up to modern times.

Taming the West: The Demise of the Native Americans and the Life on the Frontier

The most romanticized aspect of the Gilded Age was the story of taming the Wild West, complete with cowboys, prospectors, sheriffs, and outlaws. Apart from villains, it is often depicted as a world of decent men and silent heroes. One of the common themes in these tales are the "wild Indians," who are either a continuous looming threat for life on the frontier or, in some cases, even the main antagonist, trying, for example, to stop the building of railroads or kidnapping innocent women. No matter how alluring, such a depiction is far from the truth.

Since the arrival of the European settlers, the Native Americans were more or less constantly retreating westward, either by force or by will. In 1851, a number of tribes, including the more famous Cheyenne and Sioux, agreed to move west to the Great Plains. They were promised independence and were told new settlers wouldn't encroach on their lands. In return, they would allow safe passage through their territory.

Unfortunately, the native population wasn't left alone, as farmers and miners began settling on their lands. This led to a series of smaller skirmishes and wars throughout the 1850s and 1860s, including the involvement of native tribes in the Civil War. After the war, the question remained of how to deal with the still somewhat substantial native population. A commission was made in 1867, which decided the easiest solution was to once again resettle the native tribes into isolated locations and reservations. Once again, the tribes begrudgingly accepted.

At roughly the same time, Congress passed the famous 14th and 15th Amendments, which gave citizenship and voting rights to all who were born in the United States. Despite that, most politicians felt those didn't apply to the natives, as they were too wild and savage and would "dilute" the value of US citizenship.

By the early 1870s, the Native Americans had suffered severely, as their population had dwindled from the diseases brought by the settlers, constant warfare, and the lack of food. Nonetheless, at least some hoped that the new resettlement would bring them peace. However, encroachment still continued, prompting further armed resistance of the native population, which only pushed the decline of their numbers. This is exhibited by the fact that in 1870, Native Americans outnumbered the white settlers in the Dakota Territory two to one; by 1880, the settlers outnumbered the Native Americans by more than six to one.

The pushback of the constantly retreating native population escalated during the mid-1870s. Most notable was the so-called Great Sioux War of 1876/77, which was led by Chiefs Sitting Bull and Crazy Horse. The war erupted during the Dakota gold rush. Instead of evicting the trespassing miners, the US government tried to force the Sioux tribes to sell their land and leave. The natives refused, and the US Army attacked. The war remained etched in American history because of the famous defeat of Lieutenant Colonel George Custer in the Battle of the Little Bighorn. After that initial victory, the Native Americans rejoiced and returned to their hunting, proving that they weren't fighting for anything more than just their right to live in peace. This allowed the US Army to regroup, and heavy fights ensued, becoming the largest campaign against Native Americans in the history of the US. It spread over modern-day Nebraska, Montana, Wyoming, and South Dakota.

Farther south, in what is today Arizona, another famous tribe put up stiff resistance as well. There, the Apache, who, like the Sioux, had been retreating for decades, weren't willing to settle on reservations as the US government wanted. They wanted to live their lives as their nomadic ancestors had. The series of conflicts, today known as the Apache Wars, began as far back as the late 1840s. In essence, they were a continuation of Spanish and later Mexican strife against the natives. Across the decades, both the

Mexican and American governments encroached on Apache lands, restricting their way of life. As a response, the Apache turned toward raiding and pillaging on both sides of the border. By 1870, their strength had been weakened by the joint actions of the two armies, and many tribes agreed to live on reservations.

Due to harsh living conditions, many of the Apache tried to break free and return to their traditional way of life, which included raiding. The last significant resistance was extinguished in 1886 with the capture of the famed Geronimo. He fought against the settlers for decades, rising in the ranks as one of the Apache leaders. After he was caught and forced onto a reservation for good, the overall Native American struggle against westward expansion was stifled. However, small skirmishes and local fighting still occurred occasionally until the 1920s.

Apart from being cornered into reservation camps, the native population, as well as nature, suffered in other ways. With the industrial development of mining, the former panning technique was substituted with hydraulic and shaft mining, as well as dredging. The surrounding nature was devastated by these developments, leaving barren canyons across the West. Furthermore, the debris and dirt washed down to the rivers, polluting it and killing fish. Eventually, it would even reach farmlands and navigable rivers, causing issues to settlers as well. This led to the first environmental protection ruling in the US when a federal judge ruled in a case against hydraulic mining in 1884.

An environmental catastrophe of a much larger scale was the demise of the buffalo. This is often attributed solely to the settlers overhunting in the 1870s and 1880s. Their impact was great, but the larger picture tells us that the native population also contributed to their near extinction, as they adopted guns and horses for hunting and also sold buffalo meat and skins to the frontiersmen for profit. Other aspects contributed to the disappearance of the buffalo as well. The buffalo had to compete for grazing lands with the rising population of wild horses, as well as herds of sheep and cattle. The latter also brought diseases that infected the wild bison. Finally, the climate changed, and the droughts of the 1890s only made things worse. The end effect was that by 1900, their population fell to just a couple hundred.

The disappearance of the buffalo also played a role in ending the Native American resistance in the late 19th century. It was increasingly hard to find enough food, as their primary game was slowly dying out. Eventually, even the settled life of a farmer on a reservation made more sense than dying of hunger on the Great Plains. Unfortunately, the land given to the natives was often far from perfect for farming, leading to famines when the weather wasn't favorable. In the final years of the Gilded Age, the overall population of Native Americans fell to about 230,000. This was the result of diseases, famine, and continuous fighting. It is estimated that the US native population suffered a drop of about 90 percent, if not more, as estimates of the pre-colonial Native American population vary from two to up to seven million.

Yet the physical destruction of the native population was only one side of the story. From the mid-19th century onward, the vision of "civilizing" the Native Americans began spreading among the American public. This was often motivated by religious beliefs and Manifest Destiny. Then came imperialism and the revival of ideas of white supremacy. But a simpler truth is that Americans couldn't understand the various native cultures or religions; instead, they wanted them to fit into the civilizational mold they had envisioned for the United States.

The first step in this was the creation of reservations, which happened even before the Civil War. The year 1871 brought about an important precedent with the infamous Indian Appropriation Act. With this act, the US government stopped acknowledging native tribes as independent nations with whom legal treaties could be made. Native Americans were a part of the United States, but they lost their sovereignty without gaining any rights or citizenship.

The next important step in the "Americanization" of the natives was destroying their tribal structure. The US government began dealing with individuals rather than groups, which broke up the cohesion among the Native Americans. This eventually led to the Dawes Act of 1887, which divided common tribal lands among tribal members. This was officially intended to help the native population survive by providing them with farms. Instead, it simply sped up the separation of Native American lands. It was easier to force out or buy out individuals or smaller families than it was entire tribes. On the other hand, this only further broke up the tribes' traditional cultures and relationships.

Finally, in 1891, the federal government passed a law that allowed federal officers to forcibly take native children to boarding schools. The majority of politicians and the general public believed that the natives needed to be accultured to become functional parts of American society. It was believed that Native American children would be taught the necessary skills to escape poverty, with people often ignoring the fact that the government itself was the main culprit of their plight. This experience often proved to be terrifying for the young natives. They were forced to abandon their beliefs and adopt Christianity, speak only English, and forsake their native identities. Worst of all, the teachers often mentally, physically, and even sexually abused the students.

The stifling of native cultures went beyond mere reeducation. In late 1889 and early 1890, numerous Native American tribes were swept up with a novel religious movement known as the Ghost Dance. The movement was based around ideas of an honest life, clean living, and cross-cultural cooperation of natives. It was also connected with the now-famous native circle dance, and the different tribes synthesized selective aspects of the ritual with their own beliefs. However, since one of the preached prophecies was the end of white expansion, the US government saw this movement as promoting rebellion. The Ghost Dance was banned, but some tribes resisted, leading to the now-infamous Wounded Knee massacre of 1890. It marked an end to the active cultural resistance of the Native Americans, who were left powerless against the pressure of American culture and government.

A mass grave that was dug for Native Americans after the Wounded Knee massacre. Source: https://commons.wikimedia.org

The end result of the so-called Indian policy of the Gilded Age was both the physical and cultural destruction of the Native Americans. The consequences of that are felt even today, as they remain one of the more oppressed minorities in the US, and their culture continues to be largely misrepresented and trivialized throughout the world.

Sprawling Cities: The Urbanization of the US

The explosion of industry during the Gilded Age caused the boom of cities as well. New factories, mills, and other novel job opportunities were all located in urban centers, attracting high numbers of people trying to find their fortune in life. As cities began expanding, improvements were made to make life easier and more enjoyable. Plumbing and electricity benefited American society in practical ways, while other developments, like the expansion of pubs, vaudevilles, theaters, and other establishments of entertainment and culture, made life more fun. People were flocking to the cities in the hopes of bettering their lives in more than one way.

As a result, the once-rural United States, where only about 10 percent of the population lived in cities, began transforming into an urban society. And even then, most of them lived in smaller urban clusters, which rarely went above 2,500 residents. As an example, on the eve of the Civil War, there were only nine cities with populations over 100,000 and sixteen cities with populations over 50,000. By 1870, the ratio of urban to rural populations shifted to about 1:4, showing clear signs of quicker growth. By the end of the Gilded Age, in 1900, about 40 percent of Americans lived in urban centers with populations of at least 2,500 souls. The number of large cities grew as well, with 38 of them reaching the 100,000 mark. Furthermore, urbanization showed no signs of slowing down.

This dramatic shift from rural to urban lifestyles brought many changes, but probably the most important was the one affecting the social aspects of the US. As was mentioned before, the rise of cities changed how politics functioned, but together with the developing industry, a new social group of people was forming as well: the working class.

Their lives were certainly difficult. Their health and safety weren't of much concern to their employers, and they worked long hours, usually for low wages. The rise in cheaper commodities and housing, new forms of entertainment, and other advances brought by industrialization made their lives better than it would have been in prior decades and centuries, yet it was far from the quality the higher classes enjoyed. As the sheer mass of laborers grew, so did their willingness to fight for better working conditions.

At first, they began forming labor organizations and unions, which were usually localized and tied to a specific trade. It was an attempt to gain improvements by somewhat forcing their own employers and factory owners to give them better working conditions. However, these proved to be of limited success. It was recognized that a wider approach was needed. There were some early attempts at creating a national organization, like the short-lived National Labor Union (1866–1873), yet it wasn't until the 1880s that the working class managed to gain some traction.

The most massive and best organized were the Knights of Labor, which was founded in 1869 but expanded after 1880, and the American Federation of Labor, which was founded in 1881. The Knights of Labor was an organization that directly enrolled workers as members, while the AFL was an association that connected various local unions.

Their primary tool in the fight for fairer working conditions were strikes and protests. Those became rather routine occurrences in all major industrial centers during the 1880s. In the last two decades of the 19th century, there were around 30,000 strikes organized across the country. Some were peaceful, but they often erupted into violent outbursts. Sometimes it was fueled by the raw fury of the workers, but often, it was a response to the vicious treatment of the police and local law and order agencies.

In fact, politicians of the Gilded Age often looked at the labor movement with disdain, doing all they could to break them apart, even if it meant using violence. A prime example is the already-mentioned Pullman strike of 1894, as it showcased the federal attitude toward the issue. Local leaders often shared the same mode of dealing with strikes. Of course, the ties between big business and politics played an important role in such choices.

The most notable protest was the 1886 Haymarket Affair in Chicago. Workers assembled on May 1st with a "shameful" demand of limiting the workday to just eight hours. The police responded violently, even with guns, killing two protestors. The strike continued, now with added complaints about police brutality, which led a minor anarchist group throwing a bomb at law enforcement officers who were trying to disperse one of the assemblies on May 4th. Several police officers were killed and injured, and others opened fire on the masses, which included other policemen. Overall, there were a dozen dead and over a hundred wounded, and the police continued rampaging across Chicago during the night. Today, most of the world now marks May 1st as International Workers' Day partially in memory of this massacre, yet interestingly in the US, Labor Day is celebrated on the first Monday in September.

Overall, the aspiration of unionizing workers in the US proved to be largely unsuccessful. Unions did exist yet never in the scope needed to achieve major changes. However, their existence helped the workers in some cases. While their struggle for an eight-hour workday, better working conditions, better pay, and even against exploitative child labor continued well into the 20th century, many of these objectives were achieved, although some believe there is still progress to be made.

Apart from those more than honorable goals, worker unions often had a strong anti-immigration policy. They often saw foreigners as a threat to their jobs and livelihoods, and they campaigned against their arrival. Many workers even supported the so-called nativist policies of the major parties, demanding for more controlled or even closed borders.

Apart from the question of jobs, as it was true that most of the people came to the US looking for better lives, relations toward the newly arrived immigrants also depended on their background. Some of their religious or nationalist strife were transferred to American soil. For example, the Irish continued to despise the British, and clashes between Catholics and Protestants still occurred. Another part of these tensions were racist ideas. One of the most hated groups were the Chinese immigrants, who began flooding the western coast of the US. They, as well as other East Asian peoples, were usually seen as inferior to whites and often suffered ridicule or maltreatment.

The result of this anti-Chinese sentiment was the Chinese Exclusion Act of 1882, which banned the immigration of Chinese workers to the US. The act itself was heavily supported by the labor unions, who despised Chinese workers, as they were willing to work for cheap pay. Apart from that, the US government also sought to impose some rules and limitations on immigration through the Immigration Acts of 1882 and 1891, as well as some minor laws. These weren't focused on a particular nationality or race; rather, they limited entrance to criminals, the mentally insane, or those unable to take care of themselves. They also added an entrance tax to all immigrants.

Despite those laws, immigration into the United States remained high throughout the Gilded Age. As time passed, Southern and Eastern Europeans became more prevalent, replacing the Western and Northern Europeans as primary migrants. Despite that, a substantial number of Irish, Swedes, and Norwegians still migrated to the US during this time. The initial migrations from the Middle East, mostly from Syria and Lebanon, also occurred. And there was a notable migration from Canada as well.

The scope of immigration to the US was such that between 1860 and 1920, about 15 percent of Americans were foreign-born. Yet, just like the rural populations of the US, immigrants were mostly drawn to the larger cities. Thus, by 1900, about 30 percent of residents in major cities were non-natives.

Such an influx of people affected many facets of society. They brought their cultures, languages, and even cuisine. Just think of pizza, which was brought by Italian immigrants. Today, it is one of the most popular dishes in the modern-day US. Despite the pushback from parts of the native-born population, thanks to immigration, the US cities became proper melting pots of people and ideas, giving rise to the more unique and vibrant American culture as we know it today.

It is also worth noting that the rise of urbanism in the US gave way to yet another social stratum. This was the middle class, which was often composed of people who were highly educated, like doctors and engineers, as well as those working in managerial positions. They earned better pay and had "respected" jobs, allowing them to play a more prominent role in local society. This class usually followed proper manners and codes of conduct. Since the middle class worked in positions above them and received better pay, lower-class workers often saw the middle class as the extended hand of the elite, which was true to a certain extent.

Another thing that separated the middle class from the laborers was the fact that women from that strata weren't expected to work. Their "job" was to watch over the children and be a proper housewife. However, middle-class women were the ones who actually began to fight for equality. They benefited from better education and higher social positions, which equated to more free time and more respect within the community.

The movement for women's equality existed before the Gilded Age, but it only began to gain traction afterward. The initial stimulus was the post-Civil War amendments, which many women hoped would give them voting rights. Even some of the African American reformers, like Frederick Douglass, supported their cause. Yet unlike the black population, women were once again excluded from political rights. By the late 1860s, two major women's rights organizations were formed: the National Woman Suffrage Association and the American Woman Suffrage Association.

This proved to be a downside for the cause, as the two associations began competing amongst each other for influence, despite the only real difference between them being their methods. Regardless, many famed activists, such as Susan B. Anthony, Lucy

Stone, Elizabeth Cady Stanton, and Francis Ellen Watkins Harper, organized rallies and protests, asking for their rights. Sadly, their struggles proved to be largely ineffective. They lacked public support, neither major party backed them, and even some women opposed these ideas based on their religious or moral beliefs.

Their luck had a bit of a turnaround in the 1890s. First, the two organizations merged into the National American Woman Suffrage Association, providing a stronger base for their cause. Furthermore, they gained the support of the Populist Party, which led to the enfranchisement of women in Colorado in 1893 and Idaho in 1896. However, federal suffrage remained out of reach. It should be noted that though their primary goal was to gain political rights, women's rights activists also advocated for other equalities, most notably in education and employment.

Susan B. Anthony and Elizabeth C. Stanton (up) and Votes for Women pennant (down) Source: *https://commons.wikimedia.org*

Interestingly, the suffrage movement held little sway over the lower-class women. Since most of them were burdened with work, either in factories or in the fields, their activism was more aimed at workers' rights. The most notable among them was Mother Jones, who took part in numerous strikes and protests. She supported the workers' struggle for better pay and shorter hours, and she placed a lot of focus on child labor.

Overall, the Gilded Age proved to be quite turbulent and violent when it came to social change and development. Not all changes were fully achieved, some backfired, and some caused more damage than good. Nonetheless, the Gilded Age was a period when some of the most important social issues took center stage in the American public view, starting struggles that last to our modern times.

Chapter 6 – The Transformation of Life

Humankind has been in constant evolution since the first civilizations—some five to seven millennia ago—started changing the way people lived. How to control fire or the use of wheels may sound like basic aspects of everyday life nowadays, but these technological advancements made a huge difference within the cultures of our ancestors. From then on, innovations have been altering the way humans survive on Earth. Yet their introduction was relatively slow compared to the progress our lives have experienced in every field—technological, social, and medical, among others—over the last 300 years, particularly since the mid-19th century.

Many of those colossal changes happened in the United States during the so-called Gilded Age. But how did it come to that point? Which factors were combined in order to achieve such monumental progress—alongside many social issues—in this place and time? Let's examine some of the crucial aspects of this technological and scientific evolution.

Disease and Famine: Dying Young

All of the developments humans experienced in recent centuries have brought a significant difference in the quality of our lives today, yet none to such an extent as the prolongation of the human lifespan. From the 15th to the 18th centuries, the life expectancy in Europe was normally thirty to forty years. This did not mean that no one could live into their seventies or eighties, but such examples were rare. Instead, a large percentage of the population suffered from diseases and other misfortunes, cutting their lives much shorter than what we're used to today.

It was common for women to die from labor complications. There were also periodical famines and a whole series of pandemic outbreaks, such as typhus, cholera, smallpox, scarlet fever, and the bubonic plague, the latter killing practically half of the Eurasian population in the 14th century and wreaked havoc in other times as well. The case of the 1558-60 influenza outbreak in Europe was dramatic, in which an estimated 20 percent of the continent's population died.

Another poignant example of how pandemics ravaged entire communities is that of the post-Columbian indigenous population on the American continent. "The abrupt confrontation with the long array of infections that European and African [and Asian] populations had encountered piecemeal across four thousand years of civilized history provoked massive demographic disaster" among this population, explains American historian William H. McNeill. The estimates of Amerindian human losses are hard to grasp; "ratios of 20:1 or even 25:1" before and after their exposure to outsiders "seem more or less correct, despite wide local variations."

Thanks to a whole series of discoveries, medical practices began to evolve in mid-19th-century Europe. Some of them may seem trivial from a modern viewpoint, like basic hand washing. Instituting such a practice in medicine proved crucial to better the chances of patients, as it lowered the risk of infections. However, even that humblest breakthrough was a hard-fought battle.

For many scholars of the 19th century, it was hard to accept the existence of tiny microorganisms, often broadly called germs. It was seen as even more ludicrous that a germ, which is invisible to the naked eye, could cause diseases and even death. Yet by the last decades of the century, the idea was accepted and proven. Eventually, germ theory led to the development of sanitation practices in medicine, which was pioneered by a British surgeon named Joseph Lister.

Another important breakthrough was the discovery of vaccines. In 1798, Edward Jenner, another British physician, pioneered the idea of inoculating patients with a weakened virus to create an immunity to the disease. With that in mind, he created vaccines for cowpox and smallpox. Later in the 19th century, the famed French microbiologist Louis Pasteur created vaccines for anthrax and chicken cholera, while existing vaccines were improved. More diseases were eradicated or at least made less serious by the continuing development of vaccines during the 20th century.

These, as well as other breakthroughs in many medical fields, allowed humans to more than double their life expectancies in most parts of the world. Today, even the countries with the worst rates, such as many sub-Saharan countries that have been ravaged by war and famine, have a life expectancy of over fifty years; this is more than the best rates in many European countries less than 200 years ago.

However, these scientific and medical advances were a global development, as their repercussions could be felt throughout the industrialized world. The question remains, though, of how did the US exactly utilize them during the Gilded Age to prolong the average lifespan.

Both the federal and local governments realized it was their responsibility to do their best to safeguard their citizens and increase the quality of life in general. Thus, by the 1890s, most of the urban municipal governments provided their population with basic sanitary needs, like clean running water and sewer systems. On top of that, the streets were cleaned regularly. By making the environment in which people lived more hygienic, it lessened the spread of various diseases.

Following such ideals, numerous local governments also created public campaigns that educated Americans about newly discovered sanitary practices. They taught them the importance of washing their hands, airing and disinfecting their living space, boiling water for safety, etc. By doing this, the average American family became cleaner and healthier during the last couple of decades of the 19th century.

Yet that alone wouldn't be enough for a drastic improvement. The need for professional medicinal care was also recognized. It was a lesson partly learned from the horrors of the Civil War, where both sides faced a lack of medical staff, equipment, suitable premises, and proper knowledge.

The issue of medical sites was solved by building a large number of hospitals. The US had a humble 100 hospitals around 1870, and the country managed to have a more respectable 6,000 in 1900. It was a significant rise that allowed for more people to get adequate healthcare. It is worth noting that these weren't only built by local governments; in some cases, humanitarian and philanthropic associations got involved. Some were even founded by groups of like-minded physicians, whose motives ranged from pure philanthropy to the idea of profit.

At the same time, the idea of necessary medical training and the sharing of knowledge also spread throughout the United States. For example, by 1872, the American Public Health Association (APHA) was formed. It was (and still is) a body of various health professionals who shared their medical information and expertise with each other. However, this wasn't enough. Many realized that physicians needed more specialized training if they were to be more than butchers and witchdoctors. Medical schools began opening, and a major advance came in 1893 with the opening of the famed Johns Hopkins Medical School.

Johns Hopkins Medical School was established after the founding of Johns Hopkins Hospital in 1889. This educating center revolutionized the practice of medicine in the US. It introduced a more rigorous curriculum, which was focused on the scientific method, and it was combined with both clinical and laboratory practice. Additionally, the admissions standards were tightened. Thanks to such advances, which were followed by other medical schools across the country, US doctors became true specialists who could give their patients the best possible care.

Photograph of John Hopkins Hospital in Baltimore.
Source: https://commons.wikimedia.org

Alongside the doctors were the nurses. Thanks to the hard work of women such as Clara Barton and Linda Richards, nursing schools began forming in the 1870s, providing extra patient care in hospitals. It is worth noting that due to the rather sexist societal norms of the time, it was usually believed that women were unfit to become doctors, making nursing schools, for the most part, the highest reaches for them in terms of medical education.

The available medical tools also improved thanks to scientific advances. Perhaps the most notable improvement was the arrival of X-ray machines that helped better diagnose patients. However, they were a rather late improvement in the Gilded Age, as X-rays were discovered in late 1895 by Wilhelm Röntgen, a German physician and engineer. Other already available tools, like stethoscopes, were also improved, allowing for more precise diagnoses.

The advance in medicinal organizations, as well as in the available treatments and tools, managed to prolong the lives of many Americans, allowing them to reach older ages more often. However, the average lifespan didn't grow that much, as these developments had a rather limited reach, despite the growing number of hospitals and other care facilities. What was more impactful was reduced child mortality rates.

Thanks to the availability of professional hospitals, initial mortality at birth was reduced from about 170 to 123 per 1,000 births in just 15 years, from 1870 to 1885. This also improved the chances of mothers surviving births. Despite that, young children were quite exposed in their early years, as living conditions were still rather harsh, especially for the lower classes living in urban centers. To combat that, in the late 19th century, more and more doctors specialized in child care, eventually becoming known as pediatricians.

However, despite all the changes and achievements in the domain of medicine and public health, the most impactful change that brought about the prolongation of human lives was tied to food.

In a more straightforward and simpler manner, the rising abundance of various foods, from plain wheat and grain to more nourishing meat, led to richer diets, which, in, turn allowed for better health and longer lives.

These advances in agricultural output were the mixed result of improvements in technology and the expansion of cultivated lands. On the one hand, agricultural techniques developed quickly from the mid-19th century onward thanks to the work of numerous European scientists. Their research in the field of biology and chemistry provided the world with manmade fertilizer, allowing for richer yields. Accompanying that was the fact that by the late 19th century, the Industrial Revolution progressed enough to allow for the slow and gradual mechanization of agriculture.

However, for the United States, these advances were only a part of the equation. During the same time, thanks to the westward expansion, the area of cultivated land was increased. Since the nation was connected with railroads, people across the US were able to be fed by these new farms and ranches. The government realized that as well, and it sold the lands cheaply to all who were interested in working them. On some occasions, the government even granted various subsidies to aid the new farmers. By the end of the 19th century, both technology and the sheer area of farmable land improved the food situation in the United States.

The improvements in the US diet was helped by other factors as well. The railroads meant easier transport, and the introduction of refrigerated train cars in the 1880s eased the transportation of food. The technology of food processing was also advancing. People realized that by canning food, it could remain fresher for longer. While more and more companies began to work on food processing, the state also began to regulate it. For example, it ensured that milk wasn't diluted with water and that all safety and quality regulations were followed, at least to some degree.

The improvements in nourishment were beneficial to all age groups, yet it was most important to children. Thanks to all these changes, more kids managed to reach adulthood, as fewer of them suffered from diseases like scurvy, which is caused by a deficiency of vitamin C and is easily curable.

The world of infectious illnesses, famine, lack of general education, and material poverty started to radically change for good during the 19th century. Even with all the health issues that came with people overcrowding the cities, people started having better healthcare due to the many innovations and medical discoveries of the time. This, in turn, led to longer lives and an increase in the overall population. From the mid-1800s on, the life expectancy slowly started to rise. In the early years of the 20th century, people could expect to live an average of fifty years.

The Gilded Age in the United States, as well as the Victorian era in Britain and the Belle Époque in France, are great examples of how basic improvements can lead to various benefits. Many of the changes taking place within these societies during the second half of the 19th century showed the rest of the world its future, as other nations would follow in their footsteps just a few decades later.

Innovation: The Impact of New Ideas and Inventions

While talking about the Gilded Age and industrialization, the focus often remains on large corporations and wealthy individuals, as one tends to look at how major advancements like railroads or steel changed the lives of ordinary Americans. Yet the field of innovation was much wider, and it had impacts on various aspects of everyday life.

Among the more famous and impactful inventions of this period was electricity. The ideas and basic physics principles behind it had been developed since the late 18th century, initially in Europe. However, its major breakthrough in practical use came in the United States. The famous American inventor and engineer Thomas Alva Edison played a huge part in the world of electricity, as he devised one of the earliest power plants and some of the various ways electricity could be used. The most notable was the light bulb, which was another of his inventions. With it, Edison started illuminating cities across the US, starting with Manhattan in 1882; this move slowly displaced gas lighting.

By the late 1880s, another competitor came into the field. George Westinghouse, another entrepreneur and engineer, challenged Edison and his company over the electrification of the US. It became known as the war of the currents, as the two sides used different technologies. Edison was focused on direct current (DC), while Westinghouse believed alternating current (AC) was the way of the future. For over several years, the two companies competed on the market with vicious campaigns. Edison's crusades on the dangers of AC is remembered as one of its most striking features. However, AC eventually won, as it was more practical, especially for long-distance transmission.

Edison and his phonograph (up); Westinghouse (down).
https://commons.wikimedia.org

As the century came to an end, the spreading of electricity continued, reaching more and more homes. Its use was also wide, from original indoor and outdoor lighting to powering various machines and tools. A significant factor in the development of electricity was the invention of the induction motor. It was patented by Serbian-born inventor Nikola Tesla, who was a short-lived associate of both Edison and Westinghouse. The induction motor made it possible to efficiently and safely transform electric power into mechanical movement. It allowed for electric-powered pumps, lathes, mills, drills, compressors, and many more.

Many of them were simply electrified versions of previously existing apparatus and appliances. Nonetheless, the rise of electrical tools helped further develop industries and raise production. Apart from industrial use, electric-powered machines exhibited great potential for household appliances, but those would achieve a wider boom later in the 20th century.

At that early stage of electrification, steam trains remained the primary mode of transportation for longer distances. Electric trams were used for shorter local routes, connecting different neighborhoods in larger cities. As such, electricity became an important source of power, yet there still wasn't a nationwide grid, nor was it readily available to all Americans.

Nevertheless, electricity and other developments in industry allowed mass production to increase. There were more and more products made and in increasing numbers. One of the important questions became how best to sell them. The Gilded Age provided two solutions. One was large department stores, which trace their roots to large shops opened in Paris and London. The idea wasn't novel, and such stores actually existed in pre-Civil War America. However, during the Gilded Age, they proliferated, as every major city had to have one. Prime examples were Macy's and Wanamaker's. Their functionality also improved, as they grew in size and available goods. By the early 1880s, these stores offered fixed prices that were marked on every article, had flashy interiors with electric lighting, offered credits, and had themed decorations and window displays. Some even delivered their goods to people's homes.

The other solution was to take home delivery to a whole new level. During the 1870s, some entrepreneurs realized that most, if not all, items could be shipped by mail, as railroads made the whole nation interconnected. They began creating catalogs, which offered better deals than most stores since the goods were sold directly to the customers. By the late 1890s, Sears, Roebuck and Co. dominated this field of business, reaching all over the country. Their catalog had almost 800 pages, offering everything from groceries and clothes to furniture and farm implements. Due to this development, goods became available to anyone who had enough money to pay for them.

Communication was developing as well. The telegraph, an 1840s invention, was streamlined, and by the time of the Civil War, it was used for quick long-distance messaging. However, it was expensive, and the messages were usually short; thus, common folks seldom used it, mainly for urgent needs. They stuck to sending letters. Due to the expansion of the railroads, mail became quicker. This was particularly helpful when it came to the taming of the West, but it also created a stronger sense of unity from coast to coast.

By the mid-1870s, another novel invention was on the brink of a new communicational breakthrough. The telephone, which was invented in 1876 by Scottish-born inventor Alexander Graham Bell, expanded the technology of the telegraph. Instead of signaling a short message, it was now possible to talk with another person across the city, state, or even continent. Soon afterward, Bell opened his telephone company, which would become the American Telephone and Telegraph Company (or AT&T). By 1880, Bell had about 30,000 users, and the number continued to grow as more and more companies were opened. As such, the telephone began competing with the telegraph for customers. The latter remained in wider use at the end of the century, but it was clear that the telephone was the way of the future, as it could connect every home in the country.

An 1888 blizzard in New York, highlighting a number of telephone, telegraph, and electrical wires. https://commons.wikimedia.org

Another competitor in the realm of communication entered the stage in the late 1890s. This was the radio, which was developed by several inventors and scientists across the globe, but the first to put it to practical use was an Italian engineer named Guglielmo Marconi. He patented his wireless telegraph in 1896. He utilized the same signals as in the regular telegraph (the famous Morse code) to transmit messages. However, the true potential of radio waves was transmitting voice from a single emitter to a multitude of receivers, but this would be developed later on, so it had little effect on the Gilded Age itself.

More impactful was the rise of skyscrapers, which became symbolic of the growing urbanization in the US. They were a combination of several technological breakthroughs that had been achieved in prior decades. They required steel and cement, both of which became increasingly available in the US during the 1870s. Back in the day, a building was deemed to be a skyscraper if they were over ten stories. These early skyscrapers were built on steel frames and used reinforced cement. These allowed them to reach unprecedented heights. Furthermore, they required lifts, ventilation, and occasionally pumps to keep the foundations dry. These existed before, but during the 1880s, they were perfected.

The question of what was the first skyscraper is often disputed, as it varies based on definition, but the title is often given to the Home Insurance Building, which was built in 1884 in Chicago. Regardless, this advancement allowed cities to grow in height, which meant more people could fit in the same space. This was a necessity that was soon to become a dreaded reality in all major cities, not only in the US but also worldwide.

During the Gilded Age, the government, usually on the local level, began paving streets and roads, making them more suitable and smoother to ride on. This made local transport much more comfortable and faster. Interestingly, the group that initially fought for better roads weren't car enthusiasts, as some would assume. In fact, cyclists were the ones who demanded better roads at first. The so-called Good Roads Movement was formed in the late 1870s and early 1880s, as an increasing number of bicyclists demanded more suitable infrastructure for their rides. With that, cities slowly began transforming from rustic cobbled streets into cement and paved roads we know today.

Later on, car enthusiasts continued the same fight, as in the late 1890s, the first cars appeared on US streets. At the time, it was still mostly a novelty, as the first functional automobile was only constructed in 1885 in Germany; it had limitations in speed, carrying capacity, and refueling. Despite that, numerous entrepreneurs quickly realized its potential. In 1895, Charles Duryea opened the first US company to produce cars, aptly named Duryea Motor Wagon Company. At roughly the same time, a young Henry Ford began experimenting with automobiles for Edison's company; his innovative assembly line production would later come to fruition in 1903 when he opened the now renowned Ford Motor Company. By then, there were several car manufacturers in the US, as the automotive industry was gaining traction.

There were many other inventions and improvements that occurred during the Gilded Age. Some were practical, like industrial freezers, which helped with the storage and transportation of food (the home version would come later), or canned food. There were also major improvements to the printing presses, which increased the publication of newspapers and books. Others were novelties or had entertainment values, like Edison's phonograph (the precursor of the gramophone) or George Eastman's camera, which allowed for the widespread usage of photography. However, there are too many innovations to mention all, as between 1860 and 1890, there were roughly half a million patents issued in the US, making it one of the leading nations in applied technology.

Yet one thing is certain. All these inventions, both small and big, slowly changed how an average American lived their life. In just a couple of decades, their lives changed so much that in 1900, they would be much closer to our modern lifestyle than to the lives of the Founding Fathers.

(Re)Birth of American culture

Prior to the Gilded Age, American culture was mostly derivative of its European influences. It had some uniqueness, for sure, but it was usually overshadowed by the Old World. However, this began to change in the late 19th century, as US culture began to forge its own path.

It would be fair to say this "renaissance" had its foundations in the spreading of education. This can be represented in the number of high schools, which grew from just about 100 in the wake of the Civil War to about 800 in 1880; by 1900, it was all the way up to 6,000. The percentage of children attending school also rose, from about 55 percent in the 1850s to about 70 percent by the end of the century. Also, schools, which were initially only opened in urban centers, began popping up in smaller settlements as well. Along the way, some states began introducing compulsory education, furthering the overall edification of the nation.

The majority of these schools during the Gilded Age abandoned the classical form of education, which was based on higher mathematics and dead languages. Instead, they began teaching more useful skills. Some turned to vocational education, like bookkeeping and tool usage. Others remained firm in theory but became more grounded in the needs of everyday life.

Higher education was also expanding, as the Industrial Revolution improvements demanded more educated people to run increasingly complex businesses, as well as work in engineering and mechanical design. Thus, the student population saw a dramatic increase from about 52,000 in 1870 to 157,000 in 1890. New colleges were needed to house the increasing number of students, with many receiving patronages from wealthy entrepreneurs. Despite that, education, especially higher education, remained closed off to women, African Americans, and other minorities. Even poorer working families sometimes lacked the funds to send their children to school.

Regardless, overall education and literacy were on the rise. This allowed for the proliferation of newspapers, which was one's primary source of information and virtually the only mass media available during the Gilded Age. As such, the number of daily newspapers doubled between 1870 and 1890, and the number of subscribers rose even more. Apart from literacy, printing technology also played an important role in the spread of papers.

Besides delivering the news, the first mass media was also important in other aspects, namely advertising. Since it could reach an even wider audience, an increasing number of businesses sought to market their products in newspapers, and specialized agencies began opening across the US. Even politicians began using newspapers as an important way to spread their ideas and campaigns. Of course, advertising wasn't a completely new invention, as such practices can be traced to 18th-century England. Nonetheless, it was during the Gilded Age that it rose in esteem.

In the realm of the visual arts, such as paintings or literary works, American artists remained in the realm of global, or better said European, trends. This is not to say they lacked skill or originality; it is just their works fit in with general artistic movements. By the late 19th century, many of the US painters adopted French impressionism, with Theodore Robinson being one of the more famous examples. A common theme in paintings at the time were landscapes. Writers, on the other hand, were drawn to realism, depicting scenes from everyday life in a way that was relatable to readers. Another common theme in writing was social commentary, which ranged from racial issues and the effects of industrialization to corruption and underhanded politics. In this regard, there is no better example than the already-mentioned Mark Twain, whom many consider to be "a father of all American fiction."

Buffalo Bill's Wild West show in Italy, 1890.
https://commons.wikimedia.org

In all art forms, a common theme was the Wild West. Stories and images of "cowboys and Indians," the taming of the wild, and similar iconography was widely popular, with prominent examples being Jack London in literature and Frederic Remington in art. However, probably the most well-known example of western themes was Buffalo Bill's Wild West traveling shows. William F. "Buffalo Bill" Cody, a former bison hunter, soldier, and guide, created a touring exhibition, complete with numerous performers and reenactments of famed events, offering his audience "a true glimpse of the West" in their hometowns. His popularity was so high that he became an American icon, and his stories continued to influence future depictions of the Wild West. This kind of performance arts was actually where US culture began trailblazing its own unique path.

In a more traditional and classical fashion, theaters and operas were gaining in popularity, especially on the East Coast. The prime example of this is the emergence of Broadway in New York during the 1880s. It became known as a theater district, illuminated with glamourous electric lighting, and a center of theatrical activities in the US. However, at the time, American theater remained under heavy British influence, though productions started to shift to satisfy the desires of an American audience.

Vaudevilles became all the rage in the late 1870s and early 1880s. These were variety shows, with performers exhibiting numerous acts like juggling, singing, gymnastics, dancing, and so on. These shows were made to appeal to a wide audience, one that consisted of all ages and sexes. They had a bit of everything in them. As such, they reflected all the diversity one could find in a major city, all under one roof.

Analog to that was the touring circus, which provided entertainment to a much broader audience, although it was not necessarily tied to the urban areas. Circuses presented their viewers with acrobats, animal acts, clowns, athletes, and even so-called "freak shows," all wrapped under one movable tent. Of course, circus as a form of entertainment was much older than the Gilded Age, with its modern roots going back to mid-18th-century England. However, in late 19th-century America, it gained in popularity and entered its "golden age."

Another aspect of performing arts where the US found its own voice was music. Although classical music was still widely performed, usually for the higher classes, the average American began developing a taste for what was to become "popular music." The most notable among the developing music styles and genres were Appalachian folk music, blues, and ragtime, which were all unique to the US. This uniqueness was brought about by mixing several different influences, most notably African beats and rhythm, slave work chants, Christian songs, English hymns, and Scottish and Irish fiddle music. In the case of ragtime, a classical influence also seeped in, with the piano being the main influence. Of course, other influences were present, as new immigrants added to these genres. They became the base of so-called "popular music," which evolved during the 20ᵗʰ century into new genres like jazz, rock and roll, country, bluegrass, soul, and many more.

By the 1890s, the popularity of these music genres exploded. This was when the US music industry became a business for the first time. At that point, New York was the center of music publishing with its famous Tin Pan Alley, which was a collective of numerous publishers and songwriters who were based in Manhattan. However, music publishing was a much different endeavor than today. Despite the fact that the phonograph had already been invented, recorded audio wasn't demanded. Instead, these music companies printed sheets for specific pieces, which they then sold to performing artists across the US. And the demand was high, as many Americans looked for their entertainment in dance halls.

In those halls, crowds of people gathered to dance and have fun, accompanied by the sounds of various genres of popular music. In a way, these were the forerunners of modern-day nightclubs. By the late 19ᵗʰ century, it was common for every town and city to have at least one dance hall.

Apart from that, saloons, taverns, bars, and gentlemen's social clubs were places where people gathered to socialize and drink. The exact name of such establishments varied depending on social class, region, and migrant influences, but they all had several common traits. The main one was that they served alcoholic beverages, usually beer and whiskey. Apart from that, it was common for patrons to gossip, discuss their jobs and possible trade unions, and play various games, such as checkers, chess, and cards. Another common trait was that their patrons were usually men, so much so that some establishments even banned women and children from entering, at least from the front.

Temperance movements often targeted these bars and saloons as dens of evil and alcoholism. However, most of the patrons were poor working-class men, so they actually didn't have too much money to spend. The primary role of such institutions was socializing and for the leisure of working men. Because of that, it isn't surprising that by 1900, there were around 325,000 drinking and socializing establishments across the US.

The search for leisure and entertainment also led to the formation of another defining aspect of US culture: spectator sports. One of the earliest was baseball, which evolved from a similar British game in the 1840s. However, at the time, it was merely a pastime. By 1869, the first professional team was formed: the Cincinnati Red Stockings. Professional leagues soon followed, most notably the National League of Professional Baseball Clubs (the current National League) and the American League of Professional Baseball Clubs (the current American League). The popularity of baseball can be attested by the reported attendance record of the Philadelphia Phillies in 1895. They amassed almost 500,000 spectators in total that season.

A painting of baseball players practicing (1875).
https://commons.wikimedia.org

Other sports were also popular. For example, football, a modified form of soccer and rugby, had its first professional college game in 1869. A slightly later "invention" was basketball. It was devised in 1891 by Dr. James Naismith, a physical education instructor who wanted to create a sport that could be played indoors during the winter. By the end of the Gilded Age, all three sports, as well as many other "smaller ones," gathered legions of loyal fans, who watched games as they feverously supported their favorite teams. By then, sports had become an inescapable part of the entertainment industry in American society.

Finally, US cuisine transformed during the Gilded Age. There are many dishes that exemplify this, with great regional variety. However, it is likely that hotdogs (or frankfurters as they were known at the time) and hamburgers are perhaps the most synonymous with American food. Both were heavily influenced and based on German roots, and they are quick and easy to make. As such, they proved to be perfect candidates for the future development of fast food, as well as Italian pizza, which was also popularized during this time. Apart from food, carbonated soft drinks gained popularity in the late 19th century. It is probably enough to mention that one of the most famous soft drinks in the world, Coca-Cola, was invented in 1886 by John S. Pemberton. Other similar tonics and sodas appeared at the time, yet there is no other so unequivocally American than an ice-cold Coke.

Conclusion - Foundations for a New Century

The Gilded Age was a crucial time in US history. It was a period in which the United States transformed from an agrarian and rural nation into an increasingly urbanized and industrial country. It crystalized the political landscape of two major parties, which cemented the basis of both internal and foreign policies. One supported the free market and large corporations, while the other was in favor of expanding power and influence across US borders. These remain the backbone of the American nation to this day.

Socially, it was a period when both working and white-collar classes rose to prominence, while African Americans and women were only beginning to fight for their rights. These issues, along with the rights of Native Americans, which were totally ignored at the time, are issues that still plague American society.

Economically, it was a period of ups and downs, where overall production and wealth increased. Yet it was a time of great economic crises and increasing affluence disparity. It was also a time when inventions and technology boomed, leading to even more changes.

Even the way Americans led their lives changed. They began reading more, watching sports, and listening to popular music while living in cities and riding on trains and trams. They shopped more, even from their homes, while looking for ways to entertain themselves. Their lives became longer and healthier, and people became more educated.

All these changes and transformations had their good and bad sides, while some were even contradictory. As such, the late 19th century became a time of both prosperity and poverty, of rights and discrimination, of cultural demise and renaissance. Thus, they represent the Gilded Age in a nutshell.

However, it is wrong to think that the United States was the only nation in the late 19th century to have these kinds of developments. Many of the above-mentioned traits were also present in the Victorian era (1837–1901). Britain saw a renewed increase in industrial output in the latter half of the 19th century, the rise in big business and corporations, and colonial expansion fueled by imperialism. Another similarity was the fact that British politics was also ruled by two major political parties, as it was a parliamentary monarchy. Even their quality of life saw a similar rise, with the population doubling in most of the nation. Alongside that, education was also quickly developing. However, while the US thinks of this period as "gilded," most British think of the Victorian age as "golden."

Likewise, many in France consider their Belle Époque (1880–1914) as a period of prosperity and economic growth. Although it was lower than that of Britain or the US, it was still substantial. France also expanded its colonial empire under the veil of imperialism, though its inner political stage was filled with more than just two parties. However, this period of French history is mostly linked to its cultural boom, as Paris was the artistic capital of the world. The rest of the nation reaped the fruits of scientific developments, which led to healthier and longer lives.

The similarities between the histories of the US, Britain, and France might be somewhat surprising, yet there are two other nations whose historical likeness to the United States is even greater. Those countries were Germany and Japan. Unlike France and Britain, these two nations weren't major imperial powers or important forerunners in technology and industry prior to the last decades of the 19th century. Yet, like the US, they rose up to challenge them as major powers.

During its Meiji period (1868-1912), Japan went from a nation that was lagging behind the Western world to an imperial force backed by an impressive industry in a matter of decades. This was followed by the widening of education, the booming of culture, and the rise in life quality. Other similarities with the US lay in the fact that prior to this age, Japan was leading an isolationistic policy, one that was even more pronounced than in America. Furthermore, Japan felt that East Asia should be its domain, and it looked for colonies to establish in its vicinity.

The similarities between the Gilded Age and the era of the German Empire (1871-1914) start with their beginnings. Germany was unified by the conclusion of the Franco-Prussian War in 1871. Although it was not the same as the Civil War, it has some resemblances to it. After the war, Germany went through a rapid industrial rebirth, coming behind only Britain and the US by the 1900s. It was also seeking its place in the world of imperial powers, similar to the United States, while also enjoying the positive effects of technological and scientific breakthroughs. It's also worth mentioning that the German state also had a somewhat dubious stance toward minorities, particularly toward Jews and Poles, though it was not as public as in the US.

Overall, it is clear that the United States wasn't an isolated occurrence in the history of the world. By then, globalism was in its infant stage, as nations slowly became intrinsically connected and dependent on each other, which can be seen by the fact that both economic crises of 1873 and 1893 affected all the mentioned nations. Nonetheless, the United States had its uniqueness, which was mostly exhibited in its tremendous immigration, with "new Americans" coming even from all the above-mentioned countries.

One thing remains clear—the modern United States has its roots in the Gilded Age, whose importance in shaping the American nation lies second only to the revolutionary times. The practices and ideas born during this age shaped the present-day US. As such, it could be claimed that the Gilded Age was the foundation of the United States for the new century.

Here's another book by Captivating History that you might like

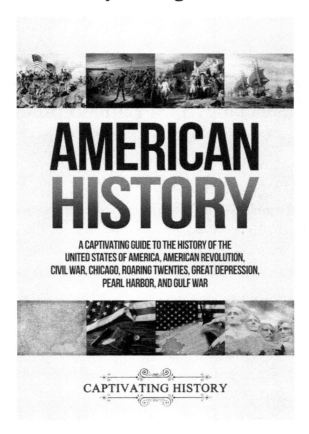

Free Bonus from Captivating History
(Available for a Limited time)

Hi History Lovers!

Now you have a chance to join our exclusive history list so you can get your first history ebook for free as well as discounts and a potential to get more history books for free! Simply visit the link below to join.

Captivatinghistory.com/ebook

Also, make sure to follow us on Facebook, Twitter and Youtube by searching for Captivating History.

Bibliography

Daniel Yergin, *The Prize. The Epic Quest for Oil, Money & Power*. Simon & Schuster, 1991-1992.

E. I. Perry and K. M. Smith, *The Gilded Age and Progressive Era: A Student Companion*, New York, Oxford University Press, 2006.

George Brown Tindall, *America: A Narrative History*, New York, W. W. Norton & Company, 2013.

H. W. Brands, T. H. Breen, R. H. Williams and A. J. Gross, *American Stories: A History of the United States*, New Jersey, Pearson Education, 2012.

Herbert S. Klein, *A Population History of the United States*, Cambridge, Cambridge University Press, 2004.

Howard Zinn, *A People's History of the United States: 1492-Present*, New York, HarperCollins, 2003

Janette T. Greenwood, *The Gilded Age: A History in Documents*, New York, Oxford University Press, 2000.

John Buenker and Joseph Buenker, *Encyclopedia of the Gilded Age and Progressive Era*, New York, Sharpe Reference, 2013.

Judith Freeman Clark, *Eyewitness History: The Gilded Age*, New York, Facts on File, 2006.

M. Economides and R. Oligney, *The Color of Oil: The History, the Money, and the Politics of the World's Biggest Business.* Round Oak Publishing Company, Inc., 2000

Mary Beth Norton et al*., A People & a Nation: A History of the United States*, Boston, Houghton Mifflin Company, 2008.

Philip Jenkins, *A History of the United States*, Hampshire, Palgrave McMillan, 2003.

Rebecca Valentine, *Gilded Age and Progressive Era Reference Library*, Detroit, Thomson Gale, 2008.

Richard White, *The United States during Reconstruction and the Gilded Aage 1865-1896*, New York, Oxford University Press, 2017.

Robert V. Remini, *A Short History of the United States*, New York, HarperCollins Publishers, 2008.

Rodney P. Carlisle, *Handbook to Life in America: The Gilded Age 1870 to 1900*, New York, Facts on File, 2009.

Susan-Mary Grant, *A Concise History of the United States of America*, Cambridge, Cambridge University Press, 2012.

T. Adams Upchurch, *Historical Dictionary of the Gilded Age*, Plymouth, Scarecrow Press, 2009.

U.S. Department of State, *Outline of U.S. History*, Washington DC, Bureau of International Information Programs, 2005.

William H. McNeill, *Plagues and Peoples.* Anchor Press/Doubleday, 1976.

Online Sites:

Antebellum era | Project Gutenberg Self-Publishing - eBooks | Read eBooks online. Dec. 9, 2020

Radical Reconstruction, 1867–1872 | US History II (OS Collection) (lumenlearning.com). Dec. 9, 2020.

Confederate railroads in the American Civil War - Wikipedia. Dec. 18, 2020.

Presidency of Andrew Johnson - Wikipedia. Dec. 21, 2020.

Question: What was the amount of South Carolina's Debt at the End of the Civil War? | Civil War History Discussion (civilwartalk.com). Dec. 18, 2020.

Those Southern Repudiated Bonds | VQR Online. Dec. 18, 2020.

The Wade-Davis Bill and Reconstruction (thoughtco.com). Dec 21, 2020.

Reconstruction and Rights | Civil War and Reconstruction, 1861-1877 | U.S. History Primary Source Timeline | Classroom Materials at the Library of Congress | Library of Congress (loc.gov). Dec. 10, 2020.

Civil Rights Act of 1866 - Wikipedia. Dec. 16, 2020.

Voting Rights Act of 1965 - Definition, Summary & Significance - HISTORY. Dec. 18, 2020.

Joint Committee on Reconstruction - Bing. Dec. 16, 2020.

Jim Crow Laws: Definition, Facts & Timeline - HISTORY. Dec. 11, 2020.

Radical Reconstruction | History, Causes, & Effects | Britannica. Dec. 10, 2020.

Black Codes (United States) - Wikipedia. Dec. 9, 2020.

Andrew Johnson, Impeachment, and Reconstruction – Brewminate. Dec. 18, 2020.

How did the South react to the election of Abraham Lincoln as President of the U.S. in 1860? - eNotes.com. Dec. 9, 2020.

Reconstruction - Civil War End, Changes & Act of 1867 - HISTORY. Dec. 10, 2020.

U.S. Constitution - Thirteenth Amendment | Resources | Constitution Annotated | Congress.gov | Library of Congress. Dec. 17, 2020.

Freedmen's Bureau - Wikipedia. Dec 17, 2020.

How the 1876 Election Tested the Constitution and Effectively Ended Reconstruction - HISTORY. Dec. 21, 2020.

Civil War - Causes, Dates & Battles - HISTORY. Dec. 11, 2020.

Books and Publications

Foner, Eric. *Reconstruction Updated Edition: America's Unfinished Revolution, 1863-18* (Harper Perennial Modern Classics). Format: Kindle Edition, Amazon. December 2, 2014.

Gates, Henry Louis Jr. *Stony the Road: Reconstruction, White Supremacy, and the Rise of Jim Crow.* Format: Kindle Edition. April 2, 2019.

Simpson, Brooks D. *Reconstruction: Voices from America's First Great Struggle for Racial Equality* (LOA #303) (Library of America). Format: Kindle Edition, Amazon. January 30, 2018.